White Chocolate

JANICE WALD HENDERSON

CB
CONTEMPORARY
BOOKS
CHICAGO · NEW YORK

Library of Congress Cataloging-in-Publication Data

Henderson, Janice Wald.
    White chocolate / Janice Wald Henderson.
            p.   cm.
        Includes index.
        ISBN 0-8092-4363-6 (pbk.)
        1. Cookery (White chocolate)   2. Desserts.   I. Title.
    TX767.W48H46   1989
    641.6'374—dc19
                                                        88-39341
                                                            CIP

Published by Contemporary Books, Inc.
180 North Michigan Avenue, Chicago, Illinois 60601
Manufactured in the United States of America
Library of Congress Catalog Card Number: 88-39341
International Standard Book Number: 0-8092-4783-6 (cloth)
                                        0-8092-4363-6 (paper)

Published simultaneously in Canada by Beaverbooks, Ltd.
195 Allstate Parkway, Valleywood Business Park
Markham, Ontario L3R 4T8 Canada

To Kary, my husband, and Kerith, my daughter—
with much love

Contents

Acknowledgments

I'd like to express my deepest gratitude to:

Joyce Resnik, who was initially hired as recipe tester but whose impact grew to encompass every aspect of this book. She tirelessly researched, tested, and retested recipes, ensuring their success for the home cook. Her creativity, professionalism, and incredible good humor made a major contribution to *White Chocolate*.

Sarah Tenaglia, for her expert recipe styling; Nancie McDermott, for her impressive research; Kit Kingsley, for cheerfully, and seemingly endlessly, word processing. My attorney, Susan Grode. Julia Wesson of Palatex, Inc., for generously sharing her knowledge of white chocolate.

Nancy Crossman, Contemporary Books, Inc., associate publisher and—fortunately for me—my editor, for her guidance and faith.

Michael Schneider, Barbara Albright, and the *Chocolatier* staff for supporting me in every way. Diane Rossen Worthington, Jan Weimer, Barbara Fairchild, Kim Upton, Joan Steuer, and Jane Lasky, for their invaluable professional and personal encouragement.

My sister Donna, my brother Jonathan, and my parents David and Blossom Wald—constant reminders that if I've accomplished only one thing in life, it was being born into the most wonderful, loving family. Assorted Walds, Karlins, and Silvermans who reside thousands of miles away, but are always close to me. The collective Bartmassers, who can finally stop asking me if I've finished this book.

The chefs and home cooks who contributed so many wonderful recipes—your eagerness to accommodate this project will not be forgotten.

Introduction

   White chocolate has had much in common with Rodney Dangerfield—it has received little respect. That is, until now. Over the past few years, there has been a steadily increasing demand for the product. Today it is not only popping up on menus of tony restaurants from coast to coast, but it is also the star flavoring of countless products: from sodas and popcorn to cookies and novelty confections in every imaginable shape from cars to dominoes. A major manufacturer, Nestlé Foods Corporation, was the first to introduce a white chocolate candy bar, Alpine White® with Almonds, that is sold on as many candy counters as its darker brethren. The popular Mrs. Field's cookies now include white chocolate variations. Even Baskin-Robbins has dished up ice cream utilizing white chocolate.

   Why the current obsession with white chocolate? To me, the answer is obvious. During the last decade, Americans have been consumed with, and increasingly consuming, chocolate. The end result is that our knowledge of chocolate has increased, our tastes have become sophisticated, and products are being developed that cater to our newfound savvy. Shops that feature domestic and European confections flourish in countless cities. A magazine, *Chocolatier*, is sustained by its devotion to this singular subject. Numerous cookbooks dish up only chocolate recipes.

Chocophiles, however, have long been left in the dark (pardon the pun) on the subject of white chocolate. Part of the problem is that it's not legal to label this delicious concoction "white chocolate" in this country. Thus, each manufacturer gives it a different name, adding to the confusion.

White chocolate remains the one untouched territory in our embrace of chocolate. Many consumers really don't know what its ingredients are and how it can best be used in desserts. And so, it's a natural progression—an evolution of sorts—that we are now enamored of this mysterious, unexplored facet of the chocolate industry.

Another reason for white chocolate's current popularity is that it's often perceived as a lighter-tasting product than milk or dark chocolate. And since today's society is so interested in eating light, white chocolate may be the chosen dessert of the new age.

I wrote *White Chocolate* with the intent to reveal as much as possible about white chocolate's composition and qualities—and to share some wonderful recipes! By the time you finish reading this book, you will understand not only what white chocolate is, but how best to enjoy it—whether you're eating it "straight" or baking a cake.

I hope those of you who are not already white chocolate fans will become ones. I believe that in many instances, consumers have snubbed white chocolate because they've either sampled an inferior quality, stale (or even worse, imitation) white chocolate, or they've tasted it used to excess in an overly sweet dessert.

When preparing desserts, white chocolate can play four different, yet valid roles—some or all at the same time. It can be a main flavoring, a supporting flavoring, a texture enhancer, or a sweetener. In *White Chocolate*, the recipes take advantage of all of white chocolate's properties. The recipes also display white chocolate's remarkable versatility: it can be incorporated into every dessert, from cookies to ice creams. One chapter,

"A Hint of White Chocolate," is devoted to white chocolate's use as a secondary, yet vital ingredient.

In my attempt to discover the best white chocolate desserts nationwide, I sampled hundreds of recipes sent to me by white chocolate enthusiasts. I'm sure I missed several winners, yet I was amazed to learn just how many cooks in this country love white chocolate and use it with skill and imagination. The recipes are primarily a compilation of many contributors, ranging from well-known chefs and restaurateurs to food writers and home cooks. They come from almost every corner of the country, from premier hotels in Hawaii to Kentucky home cooks and New York caterers. All the recipes were tested and, if necessary, slight adaptations were made to ensure their success in home kitchens. As many of us prepare desserts when entertaining, these recipes are, for the most part, simple to make, and each offers do-ahead suggestions for preparation in advance. Since white chocolate can be a bit tricky to work with, I recommend that readers review the information in Chapter 1 before making these recipes.

I would be most happy if after perusing this book, readers realize that white chocolate may be the "un-chocolate," but it is by no means a pale imitation of the real thing.

White Chocolate

1
A White Chocolate Primer

About White Chocolate
What It Is

White chocolate is composed of sugar, cocoa butter, dry milk solids, and flavorings such as vanillin or vanilla. Occasionally, an emulsifier is added. Because of its absence of chocolate liquor—the unsweetened, fat-free chocolate solids extracted from the cocoa bean that give chocolate its rich, dark color and distinctive flavor—the Food and Drug Administration (FDA) Standards of Identity consider it illegal to label this substance "white chocolate." Instead, in the United States it must be labeled "white coating" or "white confectionery." Foreign manufacturers cannot export any product labeled "white chocolate" to this country. Therefore, they give it a range of exotic names, such as "Blancor" or "Ivoire."

White chocolate is considered to be more expensive to produce than chocolate, as it contains more of the costly cocoa butter. In fact, since cocoa butter is one of white chocolate's primary components—and it comes from the cocoa bean, as does chocolate—many food professionals argue that it deserves to be legally granted its proper name.

If you travel to Switzerland and many other European countries, you'll note that in that corner of the world, white chocolate officially exists. Common European standards of identity define white chocolate as consisting of sugar, cocoa butter, and milk.

What It's Not

A simple way to check if the product you encounter in this country is truly white chocolate is to read the ingredient list on the label. Real white chocolate does not contain other, less expensive vegetable fats—only cocoa butter. If it does, it is considered to be a confectionery coating called "summer coating." Summer coatings, which are made with sugar, hardened fats, and dry milk solids, often come in pastel colors due to the addition of vegetable coloring, and they are used to make inexpensive molded candies, as they don't require tempering. Unfortunately, summer coatings are often confused with white chocolate—yet they do not possess the flavor and texture of the real thing. Chocolate connoisseurs call them "artificial white chocolate."

Besides reading labels, a fast way to check if a product is white chocolate is to note its color. Summer coatings are usually pure white; white chocolate comes in shades of ivory. Summer coatings also lack that chocolaty aroma that white chocolate often possesses from its cocoa butter content. Another clue is that summer coatings are usually at least 50 percent less expensive than white chocolate.

What can make the distinction confusing is that you can find products that boast a cocoa butter content, yet still contain hardened vegetable fats. These hybrid products are not considered white chocolate.

How It's Made

Up to a point, white chocolate is processed exactly like chocolate. The cocoa beans are harvested, fermented, and dried before being shipped to various ports in Europe and North America. Then they are brushed, cleaned, and roasted. The roasting enhances their aroma and enables an easier removal of the husks from the nibs, the meat of the beans.

The next step is to crush the beans to rid them of their husks, and then, often, a variety of beans is blended—much like when making coffee. At this point, the beans are ground into a paste. The paste is then put through presses, and most of the cocoa butter is extracted. The fat-free solids, or chocolate liquor, can be processed to make cocoa powder or can be combined with cocoa butter and other ingredients and further refined to make other forms of chocolate. To make white chocolate, the cocoa butter is combined with sugar, milk solids, and flavoring, and the refining process is continued.

Advantages

Some people who are allergic to chocolate are often able to tolerate white chocolate. In these instances, it is the fat-free cocoa solids—absent from white chocolate—that contain the allergens that offend the consumer. Those who are sensitive to caffeine may also prefer white chocolate. Although certainly the amount of caffeine in chocolate is much less than that in a cup of coffee, the amount found in white chocolate is even less; cocoa butter contains only a trace amount.

History

White chocolate was first introduced in Switzerland a few years after World War I. During the forties and fifties, a few brands of white chocolate were sold in the United States. It wasn't until the past decade or so, however, that white chocolate desserts were featured on many restaurant menus. In fact, I thumbed through literally hundreds of old cookbooks in search of white chocolate recipes. It wasn't until the seventies that they seemed to even mention the substance. No wonder few people made white chocolate desserts—they didn't have a source to learn how.

White Chocolates Can Differ

The primary reason consumers have been so confused about white chocolate's qualities and properties is that no two manufacturers' recipes are the same. Some use more cocoa butter than others, and cocoa butters themselves can vary in hardness. Manufacturers may also vary the amount of milk fats in their formula; some use low-fat dry milk while others use whole milk or add extra butterfat, for example. And since the interaction of fats with other ingredients is so crucial to successful baking—particularly in desserts' volume and crumb—you can now understand that substituting one white chocolate brand for another in a recipe means that a dessert could turn out entirely different. The color, texture, volume, and degree of sweetness could be affected.

White Chocolate in Baking

When baking a cake, for example, the amount of cocoa butter contained in the white chocolate you use will influence how much air you can incorporate into the batter. Vegetable shortening, for example, will allow more air to be beaten into it than butter, while cocoa butter will allow less. When adapting a cake recipe to incorporate white chocolate, you can take some general steps to ensure that the cake will possess volume and a tender crumb. Alternate the wet and dry ingredients. Eggs must be separated before they're added; egg whites should be beaten until stiff and folded into the cake batter.

Generally speaking, you cannot take chocolate recipes and transform them into white chocolate ones. Each recipe must be examined individually. White chocolate often contains more sugar and cocoa butter than dark chocolate does, which means that different chemical reactions take place. The only instances in which a switch will usually work is when you are substituting white chocolate chips or chunks for dark chocolate ones in cookies, quick breads, or cakes. Even then, you must be careful. White chocolate is more heat-sensitive than dark. Chunks of white chocolate in cookies, for example, can burn or become grainy or chalky on a baking sheet, which acts as a heat conductor. Thus, you may wish to reduce the oven temperature by 25 degrees to counteract that problem.

Natural Affinities

Because of white chocolate's inherent cream-like qualities, it works best in recipes that utilize dairy products. White chocolate is wonderful in cheesecakes, and it's equally sensational in truffles, mousses, bavarians, ice creams, ganaches, puddings, and sauces. You must be careful not to add too much when making buttercream—the combination of a lot of butter and the cocoa butter in the white chocolate can add up to a greasy frosting.

When testing all kinds of dessert recipes with white chocolate, I discovered that the most difficult to make work were cakes. To be sure, no matter which dessert you create, a good rule of thumb is that a little white chocolate goes a long way. It's a tricky balancing act. You don't want to add too much, as it's quite sweet. On the other hand, white chocolate's flavor is subtle, and you want it to be pronounced. One way to guarantee that its distinctive taste is in the forefront is to go easy on secondary flavorings. Citrus, such as orange or lemon, or spices, such as ginger and cinnamon, are particularly good matches as they help to balance the sweet properties of white chocolate.

Complexity of Taste

White chocolate varies in taste as well as color. Some white chocolates possess a distinct chocolate flavor and aroma which come from the cocoa butter. It's possible for some white chocolates to taste as chocolaty as milk chocolate. Some manufacturers, however, choose to deodorize the cocoa butter (to different degrees) to eliminate or reduce its flavor and to remove any off-flavors. If the cocoa butter is completely deodorized, its only remaining property is its velvety texture. If that's the case, the quality of the milk flavor becomes most important. It must be very fresh tasting. There is no right or wrong way for white chocolate to taste as long as it's clean (lacking in stale or off-flavors). It's all a matter of individual preference.

Some confectioners add citrus flavoring—essential oils and extracts—to white chocolate, using them as flavor enhancers. Vanilla or vanillin is almost always added. Although some consumers view vanillin as an artificial ingredient, and therefore a poor substitute for vanilla, many professionals believe that it is a better match for white chocolate than vanilla, as it possesses a natural affinity with dairy products.

I have included information on how to conduct your own white chocolate tasting at the end of this chapter so that you can learn firsthand how different brands vary. Only by better understanding white chocolate can you truly appreciate its attributes.

How to Melt White Chocolate

You must be extremely careful when melting white chocolate—a necessary task when incorporating it into other ingredients. White chocolate is exceptionally heat-sensitive. One of the problems is that the fats in white chocolate melt at different temperatures: the butterfats in the milk solids melt at a lower temperature than the cocoa butter. In addition, the milk proteins are sensitive to heat and tend to clump if overheated, which can create lumpy, melted white chocolate—a cook's nightmare. Therefore, it's necessary to stir white chocolate frequently during the melting process and to scrape down the sides of the saucepan or bowl with a clean, dry rubber spatula. To ensure an even melt, it's best to work with no more than eight ounces of white chocolate at one time. If the recipe calls for more, just add a couple ounces at a time until you've melted the right amount.

Although some culinary experts recommend grating white chocolate before melting it, it is my belief that it is simpler and just as effective to chop it into small pieces. It's soft enough to cut easily with a knife, or you can use a food processor fitted with a metal blade. One of the safest ways to melt white chocolate is in the top of a double boiler set over hot—not simmering—water. It is crucial, however, that no water or steam reach the white chocolate, since they will cause it to "seize" or "stiffen." Although you can't wave a magic wand and make lumps go away, adding solid vegetable shortening a teaspoon at a time might halt the process.

Another melting technique is to place the finely chopped white chocolate in a heat-proof bowl or heavy saucepan and place it on a warming tray set to medium temperature. Stir frequently until melted.

Other food professionals entrust the melting process to the microwave oven. There is a difference of opinion as to the degree of power that should be used to melt white chocolate. Some experts and microwave manufacturers claim that 100 percent power is fine. It is my opinion that it's safer to microwave white chocolate at 50 percent power to avoid overheating. I'd microwave a moderate amount, such as 8 ounces, finely chopped, for one minute and then stir. (It will not appear thoroughly melted until you stir it.) If necessary, continue to microwave the white chocolate at 30-second intervals, stirring after each interval. The entire process, depending upon the wattage of your oven and the amount of white chocolate used, should take just a few minutes. Remember to microwave it *only* until it's soft enough to stir until smooth.

If you will be combining white chocolate with hot liquids, an easy way to melt it is to bring the liquid—such as milk or cream—to a boil, remove it from the heat, and pour it over finely chopped white chocolate, stirring until smooth.

In many of the recipes in this book, you will notice that the white chocolate is used in a melted and tepid state. Tepid, or lukewarm, falls in a temperature range between 80° and 84°F. At this temperature, white chocolate best incorporates with other ingredients. At first, it's best to use a candy thermometer. After you've worked with white chocolate for a while, you'll be able to judge the accurate temperature by touch.

White Chocolate Manufacturers

There are several brands of plain white chocolate—in bars, blocks, disks, and chips—that are available to consumers, either in department stores and gourmet shops, or by mail order (see index). Some department stores stamp their own name on the product, although it's actually produced by a chocolate manufacturing firm. Note that due to the FDA Standards of Identity, these products cannot be officially recognized as white chocolate and must possess other names.

The following white chocolates are couvertures: Valrhona Ivoire (French); Cacao Barry Chocolat Blanc (French); Nestlé Snowcap® Coating (American); Lindt Blancor (Swiss); Carma Ivory (Swiss); and Callebaut White Couverture (Belgian). Couverture white chocolate contains a higher percentage of cocoa butter than other white chocolates, at least 32 percent. Callebaut, for example, contains 36 percent cocoa butter, Carma Ivory, 39 to 40 percent, and Lindt Blancor, as much as 55 percent. Many companies, however, are unwilling to reveal the amount of cocoa butter in their white chocolate, as they fear this information may jeopardize the secrecy of their recipes. Couvertures are conched (a refining process in which the chocolate is kneaded for many hours) for longer periods of time to produce a white chocolate with a velvety smooth texture. Couvertures are often referred to as coating chocolates because they are ideal for molding, enrobing, and dipping. Non-couverture white chocolates, however, can also be used successfully in desserts.

The following white chocolates are not considered to be couvertures: Tobler White (formerly Tobler Narcisse [Swiss]); and Droste White Pastilles (Dutch), which possess 24.41 percent cocoa butter.

Two American companies are now retailing white chocolate chips. Fred's White Chips are a blend of imported and domestic white chocolate and retail in 8-ounce packages. Williams-Sonoma White Baking Chips carry the Williams-Sonoma name, but are made by Valrhona. They're considered to be a couverture and contain 38 percent cocoa butter.

A White Chocolate Tasting

Because white chocolate is made according to manufacturers' individual formulas, the best way to select which one you prefer is—quite simply—to taste as many as possible! You may discover that you like one brand for eating and others for baking. You might choose one with citrus undertones for preparing citrus-flavored mousses. A white chocolate with nutty nuances might work best in a baked product such as white chocolate brownies with walnuts.

White chocolate contains milk solids with a variety of percentages of milk fats, and it often possesses a distinct dairy product flavor. Julia Wesson, president of Palatex Inc., a New York–based food and beverage research firm which conducts professional tastings, suggests beginning a white chocolate tasting with a familiarization of the flavors of many dairy products. For example, taste non-fat dry, skim, and whole milk, sour cream, cream cheese, and cottage cheese, and note their inherent flavors. Then think about their presence or absence in white chocolate.

When you actually taste the white chocolate, note whether the flavor of chocolate, which would come from the cocoa butter, is evident. Pay attention to the appearance of off-flavors, if any. White chocolate may have an off-flavor reminiscent of solvents. Cocoa fats can possess a slightly fishy undertone if the cocoa butter has turned rancid. Other nuances can include a burnt rubber or straw-like odor and a cardboard taste. Naturally, in premium quality white chocolates, there will be an absence of off-flavors. Instead they will possess pleasant chocolate, and sweet, slightly cooked but not caramelized, milk flavors, often with mild vanilla undertones. It all depends upon the intent of the manufacturer. No matter what the flavor, top-quality white chocolate will taste very clean, not stale.

Be sure to sip water and eat unsalted crackers, such as matzoh, to clear the palate of residual fats and flavors between tasting each product, otherwise the comparisons will be inaccurate.

Besides variations in flavor, there will also be remarkable color variations between brands. White chocolate ranges from off-white through various shades of ivory to a light yellowish hue. Naturally, the preferred color is strictly subjective. Generally speaking, it should be ivory with a smooth, glossy surface.

When you break a piece of white chocolate, it should have a decisive snap. It should be a clean, even break, without splintering or crumbling.

Note the product's aroma. It should possess a delicate, fresh milk aroma.

Because different white chocolates contain different amounts of cocoa butter, the rate at which they melt in your mouth will vary. Generally speaking, the lower the percentage of cocoa butter, the slower the melt. Do not simply chew and swallow; allow the white chocolate some time to melt in your mouth and pay attention to its texture. Is it smooth or gritty? Is it waxy or creamy? Is it dry or moist? It should be velvety-smooth with an exceptionally creamy mouthful. Note residual aftertastes, if any.

2
Ingredients
and
Equipment
Notes

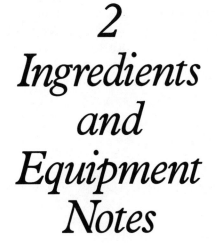

Ingredients

White chocolate: Each white chocolate manufacturer prepares its product according to its own recipe. No two white chocolates are exactly alike; they may vary in the amount of cocoa butter, sugar, and flavorings, and cannot be used interchangeably in all recipes. Thus, to guarantee their success, the recipes in this book have been tested with Tobler White (formerly Tobler Narcisse), except for a few tested with Nestlé® Alpine White™ with Almonds and designated as such. These brands were selected because they are premium-quality products that are readily available nationwide. All white chocolate should be stored well wrapped and can be kept in a cool, dry place away from sunlight for six to eight months.

Eggs: Large eggs are used in all recipes, unless otherwise specified.

Milk: Whole milk is used in all recipes, unless otherwise specified.

Cream: Unsweetened heavy (whipping) cream is used in all recipes, unless otherwise specified.

Butter: Unsalted butter, also called sweet butter, is used in all recipes.

Sugar: Granulated sugar is used in all recipes, unless otherwise specified.

Flour: All-purpose, pre-sifted, unbleached flour is used in all recipes, unless otherwise specified.

Equipment

It's my belief that most home cooks do not possess a kitchen full of gadgets or professional-size bakeware. Thus, you'll discover that the majority of recipes in this book require only standard kitchen equipment.

When you do make additions to your collection, however, be sure that they are of premium quality to ensure successful baking.

Double boiler: Double boilers can be purchased from cookware and department stores. They are crucial for the successful melting of chocolate, white chocolate in particular. If necessary, you can create a double boiler by placing a heat-proof bowl over a saucepan of hot water. Be sure to choose a bowl that will sit on the rim of the saucepan and not touch the water.

Bakeware: There are many quality brands of bakeware available today. Whichever you select, be sure that it is non-aluminum and of heavy weight to ensure even baking.

Thermometers: No matter how well you follow a recipe, it will not result in a great baked dessert unless your oven temperature is correct. Check the oven temperature with a good mercury oven thermometer on a frequent basis, preferably each time you bake. Adjust the thermostat accordingly until the thermometer registers the desired temperature. Oven thermometers are available in most supermarkets, as well as in cookware shops and department stores. A candy thermometer is a necessity for some recipes in *White Chocolate* and is also readily available.

Electric mixers: A heavy-duty electric mixer is convenient for many recipes, particularly when you must beat ingredients for a lengthy amount of time, or are gradually incorporating ingredients, such as hot sugar syrup into egg whites. In other instances, a hand-held electric mixer will do.

Kitchen parchment paper: I recommend using it to line bakeware as it's so successful in preventing sticking. It can be purchased from many cookware shops and department stores in either sheets or rolls. You can substitute aluminum foil, if necessary.

Other handy equipment: This includes a food processor, a fine-mesh strainer, a sifter, spatulas, wooden spoons, wire whisks (both balloon-size and narrow-bottom), a citrus zester, a rolling pin, a nylon or cloth pastry bag, measuring cups and spoons, a wire rack for cooling, and a natural-bristle pastry brush.

3
Mousses
and
Terrines

White Chocolate Mousse with Blueberry Sauce

This mousse possesses a light, smooth texture and is quick and easy to make.

Mousse
6 large egg yolks
¼ cup cold water
8 ounces finely chopped white
   chocolate, melted and tepid
1 cup heavy (whipping) cream,
   whipped

Sauce
1 cup fresh blueberries
1 teaspoon fresh lemon juice
Sugar, to taste

Make the mousse:

1.   In a double boiler over low heat, beat the egg yolks with cold water until the yolks form a ribbon when the beaters are lifted. Transfer the mixture to a large bowl.

2.   Beat the white chocolate into the yolk mixture. Fold in the whipped cream. Refrigerate, covered, for at least 4 hours before serving.

Make the sauce:

3.   In a food processor fitted with a metal blade, puree all ingredients until smooth. Strain through a sieve into a small bowl and cover.

Assemble:

4.   Using an oval-shaped ice cream scooper, place two ovals of mousse, slightly at an angle next to each other, onto each of eight dessert plates. Drizzle about 1 tablespoon of blueberry sauce across and between the ovals.

Do ahead: The mousse and the sauce can be made and refrigerated separately 1 day in advance. Assemble just before serving.

MAKES 8 SERVINGS.

*The creator: Andre Tripier,
former chef of San Francisco's
Cendrillon Restaurant*

Orange White Chocolate Mousse

If you like, serve this mousse with a simple, fresh strawberry sauce made from finely chopped berries, sugar to taste, and a dash of Triple Sec liqueur. Instead of chilling the mousse in individual cups, refrigerate it in a bowl. Spoon a pool of sauce onto each dessert plate, top with a dollop of mousse, and garnish each serving with a fresh whole strawberry.

Mousse
14 ounces finely chopped white
  chocolate
4 tablespoons unsalted butter
¾ cup heavy (whipping) cream,
  chilled
3 large eggs, separated, at room
  temperature
1 tablespoon finely grated orange
  zest (from 1 large orange)
3 tablespoons Triple Sec liqueur

Garnish (optional)
Grated orange peel

Make the mousse:

1. In a double boiler over hot—not simmering—water, melt the white chocolate and the butter, stirring frequently. Set aside.

2. In a chilled medium bowl, whip the cream with a wire whisk

18

until nearly stiff. In a small bowl, lightly whisk the egg yolks with the orange zest and the Triple Sec.

3. Stir the egg yolk mixture into the white chocolate mixture. Transfer to a large bowl. Using a large rubber spatula, stir the whipped cream into the white chocolate mixture until well combined. (Do not worry about deflating the mixture.)

4. Using an electric mixer set at low speed, beat the egg whites until they start to foam. Gradually increase the speed to high and continue beating the egg whites until they form stiff peaks. Fold in the beaten egg whites just until incorporated. Divide the mousse between six 8-ounce custard cups or ramekins. Garnish with grated orange peel, if desired. Cover and chill until firm, at least 3 hours.

Do ahead: The mousse can be made and refrigerated up to 1 day in advance.

MAKES 6 SERVINGS.

The creator: Michael McLaughlin, chef/owner of The Manhattan Chili Co. restaurant in New York, New York, and cookbook author

White Chocolate Mousse in Gingersnap Tulips

Ginger possesses a natural affinity with white chocolate; its spicy attributes balance white chocolate's sweetness. In this recipe, ginger is used in a buttery cookie cup which contributes a crunchy textural contrast to the creamy mousse.

Mousse
6 ounces finely chopped white
   chocolate
⅓ cup milk
1 teaspoon crème de cacao
2 large egg whites, at room
   temperature
1 cup heavy (whipping) cream,
   chilled

Tulip cups
¼ cup flour
Generous pinch of ground ginger
Pinch of salt
2 tablespoons unsalted butter, at
   room temperature
¼ cup packed light brown sugar
2 tablespoons light corn syrup
½ ounce (about 3 tablespoons) finely
   chopped hazelnuts

Assembly
*2 ounces white chocolate curls (see
    index)*
1 pint fresh berries (optional)
Mint leaves (optional)

Make the mousse:

1. In a double boiler over hot—not simmering—water, melt the white chocolate, stirring frequently. Remove the pan from the water.

2. In a heavy small saucepan, heat the milk until it is hot. Pour the milk into a large bowl. Stir in the white chocolate until smooth. Mix in the crème de cacao. Let the chocolate mixture cool until tepid, about 10 minutes.

3. Using an electric mixer set at medium speed, beat the egg whites in a grease-free medium bowl until they start to foam. Gradually increase the speed to high and continue beating until the egg whites form soft peaks. Gently fold the egg whites into the white chocolate mixture.

4. Using an electric mixer set at medium speed, beat the cream in a medium bowl until it forms soft peaks. Fold the cream into the chocolate–egg white mixture. Cover the bowl of mousse with plastic wrap and refrigerate until firm, about 2 hours.

Make the tulip cups:

5. Position the rack in the center and preheat oven to 375°F. Lightly butter two baking sheets. Trace six 2½-inch circles on each of the buttered baking sheets. Refrigerate the baking sheets until ready to use.

6. In a small bowl, stir together the flour, ginger, and salt. In a medium bowl, using a wooden spoon, mix the butter, brown sugar, and corn syrup until well blended. Stir in the flour mixture and the hazelnuts.

7. Remove the baking sheets from the refrigerator. Place 1½ teaspoons of the dough in the center of each traced circle. Place a small piece of plastic wrap on top of one of the pieces of dough and flatten it into

a 2½-inch circle with the heel of your hand. Remove the plastic and repeat this procedure with the other pieces of dough. Refrigerate the baking sheets for 5 minutes, or until the cookie dough is firm.

8.   Bake one sheet of cookies at a time in the preheated oven until they are evenly browned, 5 to 7 minutes. Cool the cookies on the baking sheet set on a wire rack for no longer than 1 to 2 minutes. Using a spatula, loosen the cookies from the baking sheet. Working quickly, drape one of the cookies over the bottom of a muffin tin or an inverted glass or coffee cup. Gently pinch the edges in five places to form a fluted rim. Let the tulip cup sit on the form until set, about 2 minutes. Remove the tulip cup and let it cool completely on a wire rack. Continue shaping the remaining five cookies. If necessary, reheat the cookies to soften them before shaping. Repeat the process with the remaining dough. Store the tulip cups in an airtight container until ready to use.

Assemble:

9.   Fill a pastry bag, fitted with a #5 star tip, with the white chocolate mousse. Pipe a large spiral of mousse into each tulip cup. Scatter the white chocolate curls (see index) over the tops of the mousse. Garnish with fresh berries and mint leaves, if desired. Serve immediately.

Do ahead: The tulip cups can be made up to 2 days in advance. The mousse can be made up to 8 hours in advance.

MAKES 12 SERVINGS.

*The creator: David M. Rexford,
the Four Seasons Hotel in
Washington, D.C.*

White Chocolate Mousse to Go

Break into a dark chocolate "bag" to discover a rich white chocolate mousse. Its flavor is accented by two of white chocolate's finest accompaniments—raspberries, in a sauce, and fresh strawberries, as a colorful garnish. Present this dessert at a dinner party for a dazzling finale. This recipe takes time to make, but it's not difficult.

Mousse

2 cups heavy (whipping) cream
1 vanilla bean, split in half
   lengthwise
2 tablespoons unsalted butter
2 large egg yolks
10 ounces finely chopped white
   chocolate, melted and tepid
1 tablespoon kirsch
1 tablespoon orange liqueur, such as
   Grand Marnier or Cointreau

Chocolate Bags

10 ounces finely chopped semisweet
   chocolate
4 small (3 inches tall with 4" × 2"
   bases) paper bags lined with a
   coated surface*

Sauce

1 pint fresh raspberries, or one 10-
   ounce package frozen unsweetened
   raspberries, thawed and drained
1 to 2 tablespoons sugar, or to taste

Garnish

1 pint strawberries, cleaned and
   hulled

---

*Note: Bags used for freshly ground coffee work well. Trim with pinking shears down to a 3-inch height.

Make the mousse:

1. In a heavy small saucepan, combine ½ cup of the cream, the vanilla bean, and the butter. Bring to a boil over medium-high heat. Remove the saucepan from heat. Remove the vanilla bean.

2. Using a wire whisk, beat the egg yolks in a medium bowl until blended. Whisk half of the cream mixture into the yolks. Return the mixture to the saucepan and cook over medium-high heat, stirring constantly with a wooden spoon, until the mixture is slightly thickened, about 30 seconds; do not boil. Strain through a fine-mesh sieve into a large bowl.

3. Whisk the melted white chocolate into the hot cream mixture. Stir in the kirsch and the orange liqueur. Set the bowl over a larger bowl filled with ice, stirring frequently until cold. Remove the bowl from the ice.

4. Using an electric mixer, whip the remaining 1½ cups of cream in a large bowl until it forms a slowly dissolving ribbon when dropped from beaters. Stir one-third of the whipped cream into the chocolate mixture to lighten it. Fold in the remaining cream.

5. Cover the mousse with plastic wrap and refrigerate 8 hours, or overnight.

Make the chocolate bags:

6. In a double boiler over hot—not simmering—water, melt the semisweet chocolate, stirring frequently.

7. Open each paper bag so that the top forms a rectangle and stand them upright on a baking sheet. Pour equal amounts of chocolate into each bag. Using a small pastry brush, brush the chocolate up from the bottom with long, swift strokes, until the inside of each bag is evenly coated. Apply a little extra chocolate in each corner. To recreate the bag shape, tap the bags lightly near the bottom of the narrow sides. Freeze the bags until the chocolate is set, about 10 minutes. (Note: Novices may wish to repeat the coating and freezing process to create a sturdier bag before moving on to the next step.)

Peel the bags:

8.   Remove one bag from the freezer. Turn it upside down and very carefully peel away the paper, starting at the bottom. Repeat the process with the remaining bags. Return bags to freezer until ready to fill.

Assemble the bags:

9.   Spoon or pipe the mousse into the chocolate bags, being sure to cover the bottom corners. Fill the bags to $\frac{1}{4}$ inch from the top. Cover with plastic wrap and freeze the filled bags until solid, about $2\frac{1}{2}$ hours. (Note: Transfer the filled bags to the refrigerator 2 hours before serving.)

Make the sauce:

10.   In a heavy medium saucepan over medium heat, combine the raspberries and the sugar. Bring to a gentle boil, stirring frequently. Puree in a food processor or blender. Strain through a fine-mesh sieve into a small bowl and refrigerate, covered.

Serve:

11.   Spoon an equal amount of sauce onto four dessert plates. Place an upright bag in the center of each plate. Fill each bag with fresh strawberries until they are overflowing.

Do ahead: The mousse in the bags can be frozen up to 1 day in advance (through Step 9). The raspberry sauce can be made and refrigerated up to 1 day in advance.

MAKES 4 SERVINGS.

The creator: Kurt Kettmann, pastry chef for the Manhattan Ocean Club in New York, New York

Vanilla White Chocolate Mousse

Vanilla and white chocolate are a perfect pairing, as this recipe so deftly proves. Be sure to allow at least 2 days to make the fragrant vanilla sugar.

Mousse

1 vanilla bean, cut into pieces
½ cup confectioners' sugar, sifted
4 ounces finely chopped white chocolate
4 tablespoons unsalted butter, cut into 8 pieces
3 large eggs, separated, at room temperature
1 cup heavy (whipping) cream, chilled
Pinch of salt
Pinch of cream of tartar

Garnish

4 ounces finely chopped dark chocolate
2 tablespoons unsalted butter, cut into 4 pieces
2 tablespoons shelled pistachios, blanched, husked, and minced

Make the mousse:

1. At least 2 days ahead: Using a food processor fitted with a metal blade or a blender, combine the vanilla bean and the sugar, and process using on–off pulses until the bean is finely ground. Pass through a fine-mesh sieve, reserving the large pieces of vanilla for another use. Transfer the vanilla sugar to an airtight container and cover. Let stand until ready to use.

2. In a double boiler over hot—not simmering—water, melt the white chocolate, stirring frequently until smooth. Whisk in the butter, one piece at a time, blending well after each addition.

3.   Beat the egg yolks with the vanilla sugar until thick and pale yellow and the mixture forms a ribbon when the beaters are lifted. Pour into a heavy medium saucepan or double boiler and whisk over low heat until very thick, about 2 to 3 minutes. Remove from heat. Whisk in the white chocolate mixture and continue beating until completely cool.

4.   In a chilled bowl, beat the cream until stiff. Using an electric mixer set at low speed, beat the egg whites in a grease-free medium bowl until they start to foam. Add the salt and cream of tartar and beat the egg whites until they form stiff, shiny peaks. Stir one-fourth of the egg whites into the white chocolate mixture to lighten it. Gently fold in the remaining egg whites until almost incorporated; fold in the whipped cream. Cover and refrigerate until set, preferably overnight or for at least several hours.

Assemble:

5.   About 15 minutes before serving, spoon an equal amount of the mousse into goblets. In a double boiler over hot—not simmering—water, melt the dark chocolate, stirring frequently. Whisk in the butter, one piece at a time. Carefully spoon a thin layer of dark chocolate over each mousse and sprinkle minced pistachios on the center of each mousse.

Do ahead: The mousse can be made and refrigerated up to 1 day in advance. Assemble just before serving.

MAKES 4 TO 6 SERVINGS.

The creator: Jan Weimer,
Executive Editor, Food, for
Bon Appétit *magazine*

White Chocolate Dumplings in Strawberry Soup

The "dumplings" are white chocolate mousse, and the "soup" is strawberry sauce. Beginner and busy cooks alike will appreciate its foolproof and easy-to-make virtues when entertaining.

Soup
4 cups strawberries, stemmed
¼ cup sugar, or to taste
1 tablespoon fresh lemon juice, or to
   taste

Dumplings
8 ounces finely chopped white
   chocolate
3 large eggs, separated, at room
   temperature
¼ cup sugar
2 cups heavy (whipping) cream,
   chilled

Garnish
24 mint leaves

Make the soup:

1.   In a blender or food processor fitted with a metal blade, puree the strawberries. In a medium bowl, combine the puree with sugar to taste. Stir in the lemon juice to taste, cover, and refrigerate at least 1 hour.

Make the dumplings:

2.　In a double boiler over hot—not simmering—water, melt the white chocolate, stirring frequently. Remove from heat and stir in the egg yolks. Transfer the mixture to a large bowl.

3.　Using an electric mixer set at low speed, beat the egg whites in a grease-free medium bowl until they start to foam. Gradually increase the speed to high and continue beating until they form soft peaks. Gradually beat in the sugar and continue beating the whites until they form stiff, shiny peaks.

4.　Whisk one-third of the stiff egg whites into the white chocolate mixture to lighten it. Fold in the remaining two-thirds of the egg whites. Using an electric mixer, whip the cream in a large chilled bowl until nearly stiff, and fold into the white chocolate mixture. Cover and chill overnight or for at least 8 hours.

Assemble:

5.　Divide the strawberry soup evenly between eight dessert plates with curved sides or bowls. Dip an oval ice cream scooper or two soup spoons into warm water and gently shape the mousse into dumplings. Place two or three dumplings on top of the sauce on each plate. Repeat the process with remaining mousse. Garnish each plate with three mint leaves.

Do ahead: The mousse can be made and refrigerated up to 1 day in advance. The sauce can be made and refrigerated up to 2 days in advance.

MAKES 8 SERVINGS.

The creator: Steve Singer, executive chef for the Hotel Crescent Court in Dallas, Texas

White Chocolate Coeur à la Crème

Here's a dessert designed not only for romantic lovers, but for white chocolate lovers, too. The traditional coeur à la crème becomes luxuriously creamier and richer with the addition of white chocolate. If you like, serve this dessert with the raspberry puree only.

Coeur à la crème
½ pound cream cheese, at room
   temperature
¾ cup confectioners' sugar, sifted
1¼ cups heavy (whipping) cream,
   chilled
3 ounces finely chopped white
   chocolate, melted and tepid

Raspberry puree
1 10-ounce package frozen
   raspberries with syrup, defrosted
⅓ cup sugar

Apricot puree
1 8-ounce can pitted apricot halves
2 tablespoons amaretto

Make the coeur à la crème:

1.   Line six ½-cup heart molds or one large heart mold with enough dampened cheesecloth to overhang edges and enclose the filling completely.

Using an electric mixer set at medium speed, beat the cream cheese with the sugar and ¼ cup of the cream in a large bowl. Add the melted white chocolate and beat until completely smooth. Set aside.

2.   Using an electric mixer set at medium speed, whip the remaining cream in a medium bowl until it forms stiff peaks. Fold the cream into the white chocolate mixture. Fill each of the prepared molds with ½ cup of the mixture. Tap the molds on countertop, fold cheesecloth over top, and refrigerate on a baking sheet six hours or overnight.

Make the raspberry puree:

3.   In a food processor fitted with a metal blade, puree the raspberries with sugar. Strain through a fine-mesh strainer to remove seeds, if desired.

Make the apricot puree:

4.   In a food processor fitted with a metal blade, puree the apricots with their juices and the amaretto.

Serve:

5.   Place a generous serving of raspberry puree on one side of each plate. Put two small dollops of apricot puree on the raspberry puree and, using a small knife, draw completely through each dollop to make a heart shape. Unmold the coeur à la crème and set beside the purees.

Do ahead: The coeur à la crème and the sauces can be made and refrigerated up to 2 days in advance. Assemble just before serving.

MAKES 6 SERVINGS.

The creator: Ruth Manchester,
The Bramble Inn & Restaurant,
in Brewster on Cape Cod,
Massachusetts

White Chocolate Bavarian Cream

You'll discover two textures within this dessert: first you'll recognize the creaminess of the Bavarian, and then you'll receive the surprise of the slightly resistant, grated white chocolate.

Bavarian
1 envelope unflavored gelatin
¼ cup cold water
2 cups milk, scalded
2 large eggs, separated, at room
   temperature
¼ cup superfine granulated sugar
Pinch of salt
1 teaspoon vanilla extract
½ cup chilled heavy (whipping)
   cream, whipped
½ cup grated white chocolate

Garnish
Grated white chocolate
Candied violets

Make the Bavarian:

1.　In a small bowl, soften the gelatin in the cold water. Slowly whisk the scalded milk into the gelatin. In a separate bowl, lightly beat the egg yolks with the sugar and salt. Slowly add the scalded milk mixture and whisk until the sugar has dissolved.

2.   Set the bowl over a larger bowl filled with ice, stirring occasionally, until the mixture begins to thicken but is not set, about 25 minutes. Stir in the vanilla. Using an electric mixer, beat the egg whites in a grease-free small bowl until stiff but not dry. Fold the egg whites into the custard. Fold in the whipped cream and white chocolate.

Serve:

3.   Spoon into parfait glasses and refrigerate, covered, for at least 4 hours or overnight. Garnish with grated white chocolate or candied violets, if desired.

Do ahead: The Bavarian can be made and refrigerated up to 1 day in advance.

MAKES 8 SERVINGS.

The creator: Alan Ortiz, pastry chef for The Lodge at Pebble Beach in Pebble Beach, California

White Chocolate Terrine

This dessert is for insatiable white chocolate lovers; the flavor really predominates. The texture is somewhat soft, but the terrine will hold its shape beautifully. Serve it with a simple garnish of chopped pistachios, or with a lightly sweetened puree of fresh berries.

Terrine
7 tablespoons sugar
2 tablespoons water
½ teaspoon light corn syrup
7 large egg whites, at room temperature
1 envelope unflavored gelatin
2 tablespoons amaretto
1 pound plus 2 ounces finely chopped white chocolate, melted and tepid
2 cups chilled heavy (whipping) cream, whipped

Garnish
Chopped pistachios

Make the terrine:

1.   Line a 14″ × 3″ × 2½″ pan with enough plastic wrap to overhang the edges and enclose the filling completely. In a heavy small

34

saucepan over low heat, combine sugar, water, and corn syrup; stir until the sugar dissolves. Increase the heat to medium-high and boil the syrup, brushing down sugar crystals from the sides of the pan with water, until the mixture registers 238°F on a candy thermometer.

2.   Meanwhile, using a heavy-duty mixer set at low speed, beat the egg whites until they start to foam. Gradually increase the speed to high and continue beating until they form soft peaks. Gradually beat in the hot sugar syrup and continue beating until cool and stiff.

3.   In a heavy small saucepan over very low heat, melt the gelatin with the amaretto, stirring until dissolved. Remove from the heat. Using a heavy-duty mixer set at low speed, beat the melted white chocolate into the stiff egg whites. (The white chocolate will stiffen as it hits the egg whites; it will gradually grow smooth as it's beaten.) Beat in the gelatin. Carefully fold in the whipped cream. Spoon into the prepared pan, cover, and refrigerate overnight or for at least 8 hours.

Serve:

4.   Uncover and invert the terrine onto a large serving platter and carefully peel off the plastic wrap. Cut the terrine into 1-inch slices and place on dessert plates. Sprinkle each serving with chopped pistachios.

Do ahead: The terrine can be made up to 1 day in advance.

MAKES 12 TO 14 SERVINGS.

The creator: Jean-Claude Berger,
pastry chef for the Four Seasons
Hotel in Newport Beach, California

4
Cakes, Cheesecakes, and Tortes

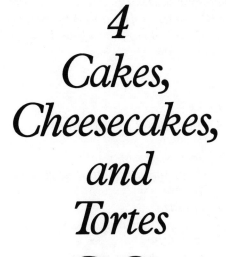

White Chocolate Layer Cake

This is the kind of homey buttermilk cake that is incredibly comforting to consume. The crumb is soft, moist, and remarkably light. It's known to disappear—along with tall glasses of cold milk—faster than you can say, well, "white chocolate."

Cake

4 ounces finely chopped white
  chocolate
½ cup boiling water
½ pound unsalted butter, at room
  temperature
2 cups sugar
4 large eggs, separated, at room
  temperature
1 teaspoon vanilla extract
2½ cups cake flour
1 teaspoon baking soda
½ teaspoon salt
1 cup buttermilk

Icing

6 ounces finely chopped white
  chocolate
¾ pound cream cheese, at room
  temperature
3 tablespoons unsalted butter, at
  room temperature

¾ *teaspoon vanilla extract*
2½ to 3 cups confectioners' sugar, or
    to taste

Make the cake:

1. Position the racks in the upper and lower thirds and preheat oven to 350° F. Lightly butter the bottoms of three 8-inch round cake pans. Line the bottom of each pan with parchment paper. In a double boiler over hot—not simmering—water, melt the white chocolate, stirring frequently. Beat in the water and set aside.

2. Using an electric mixer set at medium speed, cream the butter and sugar in a large bowl until light and fluffy. Beat in the egg yolks, one at a time, beating well after each addition. Stir in the white chocolate mixture and the vanilla.

3. Into a medium bowl, sift the flour, baking soda, and salt together. Beat the flour mixture into the white chocolate mixture, alternating with the buttermilk, until smooth.

4. Using an electric mixer set at low speed, beat the egg whites in a grease-free medium bowl until they start to foam. Gradually increase the speed to high and continue beating until the egg whites form stiff, shiny peaks. Fold one-fourth of the egg whites into the white chocolate mixture to lighten it; fold in the remaining egg whites.

5. Pour the cake batter into the prepared pans and bake until a cake tester inserted in the centers of the pans comes out clean, about 30 to 40 minutes. Transfer to wire racks to cool for 30 minutes. Invert layers from pans onto the wire racks, peel off the parchment paper, and cool completely.

Make the icing:

6. In a double boiler over hot—not simmering—water, melt the white chocolate, stirring frequently. Transfer to a large bowl. Let stand until almost completely cool. Using an electric mixer set at medium speed,

beat in the cream cheese, butter, and vanilla. Add the confectioners' sugar, a little at a time, to make an icing consistency.

Assemble:

7.   Place a cake layer on a serving platter. Spread one-fourth of the icing over the cake layer. Top with the second layer and spread with one-fourth of the icing. Top with the third layer and evenly frost the top and sides of the cake with the remaining frosting, swirling decoratively. Refrigerate. Bring to room temperature before serving.

Do ahead: The unfrosted layers can be frozen up to 1 month. The frosted cake can be made and refrigerated up to 2 days in advance.

MAKES 8 TO 10 SERVINGS.

*The creator: Jackie Bays, a
Jackson, Kentucky, home cook*

German White Chocolate Cake

This old-fashioned, three-layer cake is prepared in the style of a classic favorite, the German chocolate cake. White chocolate and buttermilk combine with pecans and coconut to make a moist, rich, and crunchy cake.

Cake

2½ cups cake flour

1 teaspoon baking soda

½ pound unsalted butter, at room temperature

1½ cups sugar

4 large eggs, separated, at room temperature

4 ounces finely chopped white chocolate, melted in ½ cup water and cooled

1 teaspoon vanilla extract

1 cup buttermilk

1 cup unsweetened shredded coconut (available at health food stores)

1 cup coarsely chopped toasted pecans (see index)

Frosting

1 cup evaporated milk

1 cup sugar

¼ pound unsalted butter

3 large egg yolks

1 teaspoon vanilla extract

1 cup coarsely chopped toasted pecans (see index)

1 cup unsweetened shredded coconut

Make the cake:

1. Position the racks in the upper and lower thirds and preheat

oven to 350°F. Lightly butter the bottoms and sides of three 8-inch round cake pans. Line the pans with parchment paper. Dust the bottom and sides with flour; tap out the excess.

2. Into a medium bowl, sift the cake flour and the baking soda. Using an electric mixer set at medium speed, cream the butter and the sugar in a large bowl until light and fluffy, about 5 minutes. Beat in one egg yolk at a time, blending well after each addition. Beat in the melted white chocolate mixture and the vanilla. At low speed, blend in the sifted flour mixture alternately with the buttermilk; do not overbeat. Fold in the coconut and pecans.

3. Using an electric mixer fitted with clean, dry beaters and set at low speed, beat the egg whites in a grease-free medium bowl until they start to foam. Gradually increase the speed to high and continue beating until the egg whites form stiff peaks Blend one-third of the egg whites into the cake mixture to lighten it; carefully fold in the remaining egg whites. Spoon the batter into the prepared pans.

4. Bake until the cake springs back when touched in the center and a cake tester inserted in the center of the pans comes out clean, about 35 to 40 minutes. Transfer the cakes in the pans to wire racks and cool 10 minutes. Invert the cakes onto the wire racks, carefully peel off the parchment paper, and cool completely.

Make the frosting:

5. In a heavy medium saucepan over medium heat, combine the evaporated milk, sugar, butter, and egg yolks. Simmer for 10 minutes, stirring constantly. Do not let mixture boil fast; lower the heat if necessary. Remove from heat and stir in the vanilla, pecans, and coconut. Place the saucepan into a bowl filled with ice and stir constantly until the frosting is cool and slightly thickened.

6. Place a cake layer on a serving platter. Spread one-fourth of the frosting evenly over the cake layer, making sure to spread it all the way to the edges. Top with the second layer, and spread with one-fourth of the

frosting. Top with the third cake layer. Evenly frost the top and sides of the cake with the remaining frosting.

Do ahead: The unfrosted cake layers can be frozen up to 1 month. The frosted cake can be kept at room temperature up to 2 days.

MAKES 8 TO 10 SERVINGS.

Robert E. Lee Cake

The whipped cream frosting adds a light and creamy texture to a Southern-style cake that's crunchy with coconut and pecans.

Cake

1⅔ cups cake flour
¾ teaspoon baking powder
⅓ cup water
2 ounces finely chopped white chocolate
10 tablespoons plus 2 teaspoons unsalted butter, at room temperature
1 cup sugar
3 large eggs, at room temperature
1 teaspoon white crème de cacao
⅔ cup buttermilk, at room temperature

⅔ cup fresh, unsweetened, shredded coconut
⅔ cup chopped toasted pecans (see index)

Frosting

3 cups heavy (whipping) cream, chilled
2 tablespoons crème de cacao

Garnish

White chocolate shavings (see index)

Make the cake:

1.   Position a rack in the center and preheat oven to 300°F. Lightly butter an 11″ × 15″ jelly roll pan. Line the bottom of the pan with parchment paper. Dust the sides of the pan with flour; tap out the excess.

2.   Into a medium bowl, sift the cake flour and baking powder together. Set aside. In a medium saucepan over high heat, bring the water to a boil. Add the finely chopped white chocolate, remove from the heat, and cool.

44

3.   Using an electric mixer set at medium speed, cream the butter and sugar together in a large bowl until light and fluffy. Add the eggs, one at a time, blending well after each addition. Stir in the cooled white chocolate and crème de cacao.

4.   Fold in the flour mixture, one-third at a time, alternating with the buttermilk. Fold in the coconut and pecans. Spread mixture into the prepared pan and bake until cake springs back when lightly touched in center and pulls away from the sides of the pan, about 25 minutes.

5.   Transfer the cake in the pan to a wire rack and cool completely. Run a knife around the edge of the cake to loosen, and invert it onto the rack. Carefully peel off the paper. Cut into thirds crosswise.

Make the frosting:

6.   Using an electric mixer set at medium speed, whip the heavy cream in a large chilled bowl until it is slightly thick and forms soft peaks. Add the crème de cacao and whip until stiff.

Assemble:

7.   Place one cake layer on a large, rectangular serving platter. Spread with one-third of the frosting. Top with the second layer and spread with one-third of the frosting. Top with the third layer and cover with the remaining frosting. Sprinkle with white chocolate shavings.

Do ahead: Cake layers can be made 1 day in advance and refrigerated or frozen up to 1 month. Frost the cake the day it's to be served.

MAKES 8 SERVINGS.

The creator: Elizabeth Terry,
chef/owner of Elizabeth on 37th in
Savannah, Georgia

White Chocolate Lemon-Orange Roulade

~~~~~

This moist sponge cake is encased in a thin layer of toasted almonds and swirled with an airy white chocolate ganache delicately flavored with lemon and orange zests.

Ganache
2 cups heavy (whipping) cream
3 strips lemon zest, ¾″ × 2″
3 strips orange zest, ¾″ × 2″
12 ounces coarsely chopped white
   chocolate

Sugar syrup
½ cup water
3 tablespoons sugar
1 tablespoon Grand Marnier liqueur

Sponge cake
⅔ cup sliced almonds
4 large eggs, at room temperature
3 large egg yolks, at room
   temperature
½ cup plus 2 tablespoons sugar
Generous pinch of salt
1½ teaspoons vanilla extract
½ cup sifted cake flour

Decoration
2 strips lemon zest, ¾" × 2"
2 strips orange zest, ¾" × 2"

Make the ganache:

1.   In a medium saucepan, combine the cream and the zests. Over medium-low heat, slowly heat the mixture until tiny bubbles form around the edge of the pan. Remove the pan from heat and let the zests infuse in the cream for 30 minutes. Gently reheat the mixture until tiny bubbles form around the edge of the pan. Pour the mixture through a fine-mesh strainer into a 1-quart measuring cup.

2.   In a food processor fitted with a metal blade, blend the white chocolate for 10 to 15 seconds, until finely chopped. With the machine running, pour the hot cream mixture through the feed tube and blend until the mixture is smooth, about 10 to 15 seconds. Scrape the ganache into a medium bowl and cover with plastic wrap. Refrigerate for at least 3 hours or overnight.

Make the sugar syrup:

3.   In a heavy small saucepan over low heat, combine the water and sugar; stir until the sugar dissolves. Increase the heat to medium-high, and bring the syrup to a simmer. Remove the pan from the heat and let cool to room temperature. Stir in the Grand Marnier.

Make the sponge cake:

4.   Position a rack in the center and preheat oven to 350°F. Spread the almonds in a single layer on a baking sheet. Roast the almonds for 8 to 10 minutes, shaking the sheet a couple of times until the nuts are evenly browned. Transfer the almonds to another baking sheet to stop the cooking process.

5.   Line the bottom of a 10½" × 15½" jelly roll pan with enough aluminum foil to overhang edges on short ends by 2 inches. Fold the overhang under the pan. Butter the aluminum foil and the sides of the pan.

Lightly dust the bottom and the sides of the pan with flour; tap out the excess. Evenly distribute the roasted almonds over the bottom of the prepared jelly roll pan.

6. In a large metal, heat-proof bowl, whisk together the eggs, egg yolks, sugar, and salt. Set the bowl over a pot of hot—not simmering—water so that the bottom of the bowl touches the water. Continue whisking the mixture until the sugar has dissolved and the mixture is warm to the touch, about 3 to 4 minutes. Remove the bowl from the hot water.

7. Using an electric mixer set at medium-high speed, beat the mixture until it has tripled in volume and the batter is a pale yellow and forms a thick ribbon when the beaters are lifted, about 5 to 7 minutes. Beat in the vanilla. Sift 2 tablespoons of the flour over the batter and fold in gently. Repeat sifting and folding process with remaining flour. Pour the batter into the prepared pan and spread it in an even layer, being careful not to disturb the almonds coating the bottom of the pan. Gently tap the pan on the surface of a work table to release any large air bubbles.

8. Bake until the center of the cake springs back when lightly pressed, about 15 to 17 minutes. Transfer the cake in the pan to a wire rack and cool for 10 minutes. Pull out the aluminum foil ends and use them as handles to transfer the cake to a large wire rack. Cool the cake completely.

9. Using your fingers or a small knife, carefully peel off the soft, brown, paper-thin layer from the surface of the sponge cake. Place a flat baking sheet over the sponge cake and invert. Gently loosen the aluminum foil, keeping it in one piece, and leave it in place on the sponge cake. Invert the sponge cake again onto another flat baking sheet so that the almond coating is on the bottom.

Assemble:

10. Brush the sugar syrup evenly over the top of the sponge cake.

11. Using an electric mixer set at medium speed, beat the chilled ganache until it is thick enough to spread, about 15 to 30 seconds. Do not overbeat or the texture will become grainy.

12. Fit a pastry bag with a #2 star tip and fill with ¾ cup of ganache. Using a cake spatula, spread the remaining ganache in an even layer over the top of the sponge cake. Using the aluminum foil as a guide, roll the roulade (starting at one short end) into a tight cylinder. Remove the aluminum foil. Transfer the roulade, seam side down, to a rectangular serving platter.

Decorate:

13. Pipe twelve medium swirled rosettes evenly spaced along the top of the roulade. Pipe a thin line of ganache down the length of the roulade on each side of the rosettes.

14. With a small knife, cut six triangles from each strip of lemon and orange zest. Insert a lemon and an orange triangle, standing up, halfway into each of the rosettes. Refrigerate the roulade, loosely covered. Let sit at room temperature up to 20 minutes before serving.

Do ahead: The roulade can be made and refrigerated up to 1 day in advance.

MAKES 12 SERVINGS.

The creator: Adrienne Welch, test kitchen director for Chocolatier *magazine, creator of Adrienne's Truffles, and cookbook author*

Strawberry Shortcake
with White Chocolate Chantilly

Fresh-baked biscuits are filled with white chocolate chantilly and strawberry slices. The shortcakes are drizzled with fresh strawberry sauce that's laced with Grand Marnier, and sprinkled with white chocolate shavings.

Chantilly
1½ cups chilled heavy (whipping) cream
6 ounces finely chopped white chocolate, melted and tepid

Shortcake
1⅔ cups cake flour
Pinch of salt
4 teaspoons baking powder
3 tablespoons confectioners' sugar

6 tablespoons unsalted butter, at room temperature
1 large egg, at room temperature
½ cup milk

Sauce
4 pints fresh strawberries, stemmed and hulled
½ cup Grand Marnier liqueur

Garnish
White chocolate shavings (see index)

Make the chantilly:

1.   Using an electric mixer set at medium-high speed, whip the cream in a chilled bowl until soft peaks form. Gradually pour in the white chocolate and whip until nearly stiff. Cover and refrigerate at least 4 hours.

Make the shortcake:

2.   Position a rack in the center and preheat oven to 400°F. Line a baking sheet with parchment paper (or use a nonstick baking sheet). Into a

large bowl, sift the cake flour, salt, baking powder, and confectioners' sugar. Using two knives or a pastry cutter, cut in the butter, piece by piece, until the mixture resembles fine meal.

3. In a small bowl, combine the egg and the milk. Form a well in the dry ingredients and pour the egg mixture into the center. Gently stir to blend. Carefully roll the dough on a floured surface to a thickness of 1 inch. Using a 2½-inch biscuit or cookie cutter, or rim of a glass, cut out twelve biscuits. Reroll dough scraps as necessary.

4. Transfer the biscuits to the prepared baking sheet and bake until color is light golden and the edges are firm but the center is slightly soft, about 10 minutes. Transfer the biscuits on the baking sheet to a wire rack to cool. When completely cool, split in half horizontally.

Make the sauce:

5. Finely chop half of the strawberries and combine in a large bowl with the Grand Marnier. Slice the remaining strawberries and reserve.

Assemble:

6. Place the bottom halves of the biscuits on small dessert plates. Top each with about 2 tablespoons of the chantilly and an equal amount of the sliced strawberries. Cover with the top of the biscuit. Spoon some sauce over each biscuit and let it drizzle down the sides. Sprinkle white chocolate shavings over each serving.

Do ahead: The chantilly can be made and refrigerated up to 2 days in advance. The shortcake can be made up to 8 hours in advance. The sauce can be made and refrigerated up to 2 days in advance.

MAKES 12 SERVINGS.

*The creator: Michael Kornick, chef
of Gordon restaurant in Chicago, Illinois*

White Chocolate Pound Cake

∽⟡∼

This is the kind of rich, simple cake that draws you back into the kitchen for just one more slice. It's delicious on its own, or you can serve it with fresh berries, softly whipped cream, or White Chocolate Ice Cream (see index).

Cake
1 tablespoon finely chopped pecans
½ pound unsalted butter, at room
    temperature
2 cups sugar
1 cup heavy (whipping) cream
4 ounces finely chopped white
    chocolate, melted and tepid
6 large eggs, at room temperature
3 cups flour
½ teaspoon salt
¼ teaspoon baking soda

Garnish
Confectioners' sugar

1.   Position a rack in the center and preheat oven to 300°F. Butter a 10-inch fluted tube pan. Dust with flour; tap out the excess. Sprinkle the pecans over the bottom.

2.   Using an electric mixer set at medium speed, beat the butter in

a large bowl until light and fluffy, then add the sugar, 1 cup at a time, beating well after each addition.

3.   Blend in the cream and white chocolate. Add the eggs, one at a time, beating well after each addition. Into a large bowl, sift the flour with the salt and baking soda. Mix the flour mixture into the cream mixture, 1 cup at a time, just until blended.

4.   Pour the batter into the prepared pan and bake until a cake tester inserted in the center of the cake comes out clean, about 1 hour and 15 minutes to 1 hour and 30 minutes. Transfer the cake in the pan to a wire rack and cool 15 minutes. Loosen the cake from the edges of the pan with a metal spatula and invert onto the wire rack. Cool completely. Through a fine-mesh sieve, sprinkle confectioners' sugar over the top of the cake. Store at room temperature, wrapped airtight.

Do ahead: The pound cake can be made up to 1 week in advance or frozen up to 1 month.

MAKES 10 SERVINGS.

Bittersweet Chocolate Cake with White Chocolate Mousse

An ultrathin layer of intensely chocolaty cake is crowned with a voluminous layer of white chocolate mousse.

Cake

5 ounces finely chopped bittersweet chocolate

10 tablespoons unsalted butter

5 large egg yolks, at room temperature

½ cup sugar

3 large egg whites, at room temperature

Mousse

8 ounces finely chopped white chocolate

6 large egg yolks, at room temperature

4 tablespoons unsalted butter, at room temperature

2 cups heavy (whipping) cream, chilled

Garnish

Cocoa powder (preferably Dutch process)

White chocolate shavings (optional) (see index)

Make the cake:

1. Position a rack in the center and preheat oven to 300°F. Lightly butter the bottom and sides of a 9-inch round cake pan. Line the bottom of the pan with parchment paper. Dust with flour; tap out the excess.

2. In a double boiler over hot—not simmering—water, melt the

54

chocolate and butter, stirring frequently to blend. Using an electric mixer set at medium speed, beat the egg yolks and sugar in a large bowl until a ribbon forms when the beaters are lifted. Gradually blend the chocolate mixture into the egg yolk mixture.

3. Using an electric mixer set at low speed, beat the egg whites in a grease-free medium bowl until they start to foam. Gradually increase the speed to high and continue beating the egg whites until they form soft peaks. Fold one-fourth of the beaten egg whites into the chocolate mixture to lighten it, then carefully fold in the remaining egg whites. Pour into the prepared pan.

4. Bake the cake until it springs back when lightly touched in the center, about 1 hour and 10 minutes. Transfer the cake in the pan to a wire rack. Let cool for 10 minutes, then invert onto the rack. Let the cake cool completely. (The center will sink as it cools.) Peel off the parchment paper. Cover and refrigerate the cake for at least 2 hours.

Make the mousse:

5. In a double boiler over hot—not simmering—water, melt the white chocolate, stirring frequently. In another double boiler, or in a heat-proof bowl set in a pan of barely simmering water, beat the egg yolks until pale and thickened. Remove the bowl from the water and continue to beat, using an electric mixer set at high speed, until the egg mixture forms a thick ribbon when the beaters are lifted. Blend the egg yolk mixture into the white chocolate.

6. Blend the butter into the white chocolate mixture, 1 tablespoon at a time. Using an electric mixer set at medium-high speed, whip the cream in a medium bowl until it forms soft peaks. Fold one-fourth of the cream into the white chocolate mixture to lighten it, then gently fold in the remaining cream. Cover and refrigerate the mousse.

Assemble:

7. Remove the cake from the refrigerator and carefully scrape away any blistered crust. Place right side up on an 8-inch cardboard circle and trim the edges with a serrated knife. Using two large pieces of aluminum

foil, fold each one over as many times as necessary to form a strip three inches wide. Staple or tape one end of the two strips together and wrap around the cake to form a collar. Staple or tape the loose ends together.

8. Gently spoon the mousse over the cake. Using a metal spatula, smooth the top of the cake to evenly meet the collar. Refrigerate 24 hours.

9. Carefully remove the foil collar. Using a metal spatula dipped in hot water and wiped dry, smooth the sides of the cake. Sift cocoa powder evenly and generously over the top of the cake. Place white chocolate shavings over the center of the cake, if desired.

Do ahead: The cake can be made and refrigerated up to 2 days in advance. Garnish before serving.

MAKES 10 SERVINGS.

The creator: Mark Filippo, chef of Jillyflower's in Harrison, New York

Blonde Bombshell

❦

Shaped like a classic bombe, this dessert features a skinny layer of white chocolate cake which encases a delicate, rum-flavored white chocolate mousse. Frankly, this bombshell is a knockout.

Shell

¼ pound unsalted butter
9 ounces finely chopped white
    chocolate
2 large eggs, at room temperature
½ cup sugar
1 teaspoon vanilla extract
1 cup flour

Filling

6 tablespoons unsalted butter
6 ounces finely chopped white
    chocolate
4 large eggs, separated, at room
    temperature
¾ cup sugar
¼ cup rum
1 envelope unflavored gelatin
1½ cups heavy (whipping) cream,
    whipped to soft peaks
3 tablespoons confectioners' sugar

Make the shell:

1.   Position a rack in the center and preheat oven to 350°F. Lightly butter the bottom and sides of an 11″ × 17″ jelly roll pan. Line the pan with parchment paper so that the paper overhangs each end by about 1 inch. Dust the pan with flour; tap out the excess. In a heavy medium saucepan over low heat, melt the butter. Remove the saucepan from the heat, add the white chocolate, and stir until the white chocolate is melted and smooth.

2.   Using an electric mixer set at medium speed, beat the eggs and the sugar in a medium bowl until thick and light. Beat in the white chocolate mixture and vanilla until well blended. Add the flour and stir until combined. Using a rubber spatula, spread the batter evenly into the prepared pan. The layer will be very thin. Bake until a cake tester inserted in the center comes out clean, about 20 minutes. Transfer the cake in the pan to a wire rack and let cool for 10 minutes, then invert the cake onto a clean, flat surface and carefully peel off the paper.

3.   Line a 6-cup glass bowl with enough plastic wrap to overhang the edges by at least 1 inch. Measure the diameter of the bottom of the bowl and cut out a same-size circle of the cake, working from one corner of the cake. Fit it into the bottom of the bowl. Measure the circumference and depth of the bowl and cut out a rectangle of cake of that proportion. Fit it into the bowl, starting at the base of the cake and wrapping it around the sides. (The cake is very flexible and will not tear.) If necessary, patch any holes with cake pieces cut to size. Save any large cake pieces to cover the bombe. Place the small scraps and hard edges into a food processor fitted with a metal blade and process, using on–off pulses, until contents resemble fine crumbs. Set aside 1 cup of crumbs.

Make the filling:

4.   In a heavy medium saucepan over low heat, melt the butter. Remove the saucepan from the heat, add the white chocolate, and stir until melted and smooth.

5.   Using an electric mixer set at medium speed, beat the egg yolks and sugar in a large bowl until a thick ribbon forms when beaters are lifted. Beat in the white chocolate mixture until well blended. Pour the rum into a heat-proof cup, then add the gelatin and let it soften. Place the cup in a pan of barely simmering water, stirring until the gelatin dissolves, about 1 minute, then add to the white chocolate mixture, mixing well. Fold in the reserved cup of crumbs. Fold half of the whipped cream into the white chocolate mixture to lighten it, then fold in the remaining cream.

6. Using an electric mixer set at low speed, beat the egg whites in a grease-free small bowl until they start to foam. Gradually increase the speed to high and continue beating until the egg whites form stiff peaks. Fold one-fourth of the beaten egg whites into the mousse to lighten it, then fold in the remaining egg whites. Spoon the filling into the prepared mold, cover with leftover pieces of cake, and refrigerate until completely set, at least 4 hours.

Assemble:

7. Invert the bombe onto a large serving platter and carefully peel off the plastic wrap. Sift the confectioners' sugar over the top of the bombe. Untwist a wire hanger and straighten it. Heat a 6-inch strip of the hanger over a gas flame until it is red-hot. Starting at one end of the sugar-coated top, use this makeshift "branding iron" to caramelize a straight line down the center and down the other side of the bombe. You may have to reheat the hanger periodically. Repeat the process by caramelizing another line across the center of the cake at a right angle to the first. Burn in two more lines so that they form a pattern of eight equal wedges. Cut the cake with a sharp knife, using a sawing motion.

Do ahead: The bombe can be made and refrigerated up to 2 days in advance.

MAKES 16 SERVINGS.

The creator: Samantha Fox,
a Los Angeles–based caterer
and food writer

Gâteau Charlene Blanche

∽∾

This dessert is a real showstopper: layers of genoise alternate with layers of white chocolate mousse and strawberries. The cake is encircled with ladyfingers and tied with a red ribbon. White chocolate-dipped strawberries and rosettes add a crowning touch. Best of all, it can be made 1 day in advance and decorated a few hours before serving—a perfect finale for a dinner party.

Genoise
5 large eggs
6 large egg yolks
1 cup sugar
Pinch of salt
1½ cups cake flour
3 tablespoons unsalted butter, melted
   and tepid

Syrup
½ cup water
⅓ cup sugar
⅓ cup Grand Marnier liqueur

Mousse
3 cups heavy (whipping) cream
1 pound coarsely chopped white
   chocolate

Assembly
1 cup sliced strawberries
20 to 24 ladyfingers, homemade or
  store-bought
3½ feet red ribbon
8 ounces coarsely chopped white
  chocolate
8 medium strawberries, cleaned and
  hulled

Make the genoise:
1. Position a rack in the center and preheat oven to 350°F. Lightly butter and flour two 9-inch round cake pans.
2. In a large metal mixing bowl, whisk together the eggs, yolks, sugar, and salt. Set the bowl over a pot of simmering water. Do not let the bottom of the bowl touch the water. Continue whisking the mixture until it is frothy and very hot (130°F).
3. Remove the bowl from the water. Using an electric mixer, beat the mixture at medium speed until it has tripled in volume and the batter forms a thick, pale yellow ribbon when the beaters are lifted, about 5 minutes.
4. Sift one-third of the flour over the batter. Using a large rubber spatula, briskly but gently fold in the flour. Repeat the sifting and folding process in two more additions. Do not overmix. Fold in the cooled butter. Divide the batter evenly between the two prepared pans and spread evenly.
5. Bake until the genoise springs back when lightly touched and the cakes have pulled away from the sides of the pans, about 30 minutes. Invert the layers onto a wire rack and cool completely.
Make the syrup:
6. In a heavy small saucepan, combine the water and sugar. Stir

over medium heat until the sugar dissolves. Bring the syrup to a boil. Pour into a small bowl and let cool. Stir in the Grand Marnier.

Make the mousse:

7.   In a heavy small saucepan, bring 1 cup of heavy cream to a boil. Remove from heat.

8.   In a food processor, finely chop the white chocolate. Pour the hot cream through the feed tube while the machine is running. Process the mixture until smooth, about 20 seconds.

9.   Pour the mixture into a large metal mixing bowl. Cover and refrigerate until it is completely cold and has started to thicken, stirring occasionally, about 45 minutes.

10.   In a chilled mixing bowl, whip the remaining 2 cups of heavy cream until a slowly dissolving ribbon forms when the beaters are lifted. Stir one-third of the whipped cream into the chilled white chocolate mixture. Fold in the remaining cream until blended.

Assemble:

11.   With a serrated knife, trim the tops of the two genoises to make the layers flat.

12.   Place one genoise layer cut side up onto a cardboard circle or a serving plate. Using a pastry brush, brush half of the syrup over the cake layer. Using two large pieces of aluminum foil, fold each one over as many times as necessary to form a strip 6 inches wide. Staple or tape one end of the two strips together and wrap around the cake to form a collar. Staple or tape the loose ends together.

13.   Spread a ¼-inch layer of white chocolate mousse over the syrup-covered layer. Arrange the sliced strawberries on top of the mousse. Spread a thin layer of the mousse over the berries.

14.   Place the second genoise layer on top of the filling. Brush this layer with the remaining syrup.

15.   Remove the foil collar. Reserving 1 cup of the mousse for piping, use a metal spatula to smooth the remaining mousse over the top and sides of the cake. Refrigerate at least 6 hours or overnight.

16.   Press the ladyfingers, with the rounded sides facing out, upright onto the sides of the cake. Tie the ribbon around the ladyfingers.

17.   Fit a pastry bag with a #4 star tip, then fill with the reserved mousse. Pipe eight rosettes around the top edge of the cake. Refrigerate.

18.   In a double boiler over hot—not simmering—water, melt the white chocolate, stirring frequently until smooth. Remove from heat.

19.   One at a time, dip the points of each strawberry halfway into the white chocolate. Let the excess white chocolate drip off and place the berries directly onto the cake between each rosette. Refrigerate the cake until serving time.

Do ahead: The cake can be made up to 1 day in advance through Step 15. Decorate the cake up to 4 hours before serving.

MAKES 12 SERVINGS.

The creator: Madeleine Lanciani,
owner of Patisserie Lanciani
in New York, New York

White Chocolate Cheesecake with Dark Chocolate Crust

This cake is quite creamy and will not appear done when it's removed from the oven. Be careful not to overbake it—it becomes firm as it cools.

Cheesecake

1½ cups ground chocolate sandwich cookies, such as Oreos (about 14 cookies)

5 tablespoons plus 1 teaspoon unsalted butter, at room temperature

30 ounces finely chopped white chocolate

1½ pounds cream cheese, at room temperature

1 cup heavy (whipping) cream

3 large eggs, at room temperature

2 tablespoons unsalted butter, melted

2 teaspoons vanilla extract

Garnish

3 ounces white chocolate shavings (see index)

Fresh mint or berries

1.   Combine cookie crumbs and softened butter and press firmly onto the bottom of 9-inch springform pan. Refrigerate. Melt 8 ounces of white chocolate in double boiler over hot—not simmering—water, stirring

64

frequently. Pour melted white chocolate evenly over crust. Refrigerate to harden, about 15 minutes.

2. Place a rack in the center and preheat oven to 325° F. Combine the cream cheese, cream, eggs, melted butter, and vanilla. Melt remaining chopped white chocolate in a double boiler over hot—not simmering—water, stirring frequently; add to the cream cheese mixture. Stir to combine.

3. Pour the cream cheese mixture into the prepared pan and bake for 15 minutes. Cover loosely with aluminum foil. Bake 55 minutes longer. The cheesecake will not appear done; it will still jiggle when the oven rack is gently moved. Open the oven door, turn off the heat, and allow the cheesecake to cool for 30 minutes before moving. Transfer in the pan to a wire rack and cool completely.

4. Gently pile the white chocolate shavings (see index) onto the center of the cake and garnish the middle with a few mint leaves or berries. Refrigerate at least 1 hour before serving.

Do ahead: This cake can be made and refrigerated up to 2 days in advance. Bring to room temperature before serving.

MAKES 10 TO 12 SERVINGS.

The creator: Kim Upton, editor for
FoodStyles Feature Service, of the
Los Angeles Times Syndicate,
and coauthor of three cookbooks
with Bev Bennett

White Chocolate Lemon Cheesecake

≈≈≈

The lemon adds just enough tang to balance the sweetness of white chocolate and the richness of cream cheese. For a simpler variation, you can serve this cake without the glaze and garnish—it's equally delicious.

Crust
4½ ounces (about 1½ cups) finely crushed chocolate wafer cookies
5 tablespoons unsalted butter, melted

Filling
8 ounces finely chopped white chocolate
½ cup heavy (whipping) cream
1½ pounds cream cheese, at room temperature
1½ cups sugar
4 large eggs, at room temperature
⅓ cup freshly squeezed lemon juice
1 tablespoon grated lemon zest
1 teaspoon vanilla extract

½ teaspoon lemon extract
¼ cup white rum (optional)

Garnish
3 large lemons
1 cup sugar
½ cup water

Glaze
6 ounces finely chopped bittersweet chocolate
1 ounce finely chopped unsweetened chocolate
2 tablespoons light corn syrup
3 tablespoons unsalted butter, at room temperature

Make the crust:
1. Position a rack in the center and preheat oven to 350°F. Lightly

butter the bottom and sides of a 10-inch springform pan. Line the bottom of the pan with parchment paper.

2. In a medium bowl, combine the cookie crumbs and melted butter. Stir the mixture with a wooden spoon until it is well blended. Press the mixture evenly into the bottom of the springform pan. Refrigerate.

Make the filling:

3. In a double boiler over hot—not simmering—water, melt the white chocolate with the cream, stirring frequently. Remove the pan from the water and allow the mixture to cool for 10 minutes, stirring occasionally.

4. Using an electric mixer set at high speed, beat the cream cheese with the sugar in a large bowl until it is light and fluffy. Beat in the cooled white chocolate mixture until well combined. Add the eggs, one at a time, beating well after each addition. Beat in the lemon juice, lemon zest, vanilla, lemon extract, and the rum until well combined. Pour the filling into the chilled crust.

5. Bake until the cake is barely set in the center, about 1 hour and 10 minutes. Transfer the cake in the pan to a wire rack. Run a sharp knife around the edge of the cake to loosen it from the sides of the pan. Cool the cake completely. Release the sides of the springform pan. Refrigerate the cheesecake until firm, about 1 to 2 hours. Insert a large metal cake spatula between the crust and the bottom of the springform pan to loosen. With two large cake spatulas, lift the cake off the bottom of the springform and place it on a 10-inch cardboard cake circle. Set the cake with the cardboard circle on a wire rack over a baking sheet.

Make the garnish:

6. With a vegetable peeler, remove strips of zest from the lemons, avoiding the white pith underneath. With a sharp knife, cut the zest into $2'' \times \frac{1}{16}''$ pieces. Place the strips in a small saucepan filled with cold water. Bring the water to a boil over medium-high heat, and continue boiling until the strips are tender, about 10 minutes. Drain the lemon zest strips, rinse under cold water, and drain again. Drain the strips on paper towels.

7. In a heavy small saucepan over medium heat, combine the sugar

and water. Stir until the sugar dissolves. Increase the heat to medium-high and boil the syrup, brushing down the sugar crystals from the sides of the pan with water, until the mixture registers 238°F on a candy thermometer. Remove the pan from heat. Stir in the lemon zest. Let the lemon zest soak in the syrup for at least 1 hour.

Make the glaze:

8.   In a double boiler over hot—not simmering—water, melt the bittersweet and unsweetened chocolates with the corn syrup, stirring frequently. Remove the pan from the water and stir in the butter, 1 tablespoon at a time, mixing well after each addition.

Assemble:

9.   Spoon the warm glaze over the top of the cheesecake. Using a large cake spatula, spread the glaze over the top of the cake, letting the excess glaze run down the sides. Smooth the glaze over the top and the sides of the cake. Arrange the lemon zest garnish in a circle around the edges of the cake. Refrigerate the cake until the glaze is set, about 1 hour.

Do ahead: The cheesecake can be made and refrigerated up to 1 day in advance.

MAKES 10 SERVINGS.

The creator: Gayle Feyrer, northern
California resident and winner with
this recipe of second prize in
Chocolatier *magazine's annual*
Great Chocolate Challenge

White Chocolate Cheesecake

It would be hard to find a pure white chocolate cheesecake better than this one—it's textbook perfect.

Crust
1¾ cups graham cracker crumbs
  (about 16 crackers)
6 tablespoons unsalted butter, melted
1 tablespoon sugar

Filling
10 ounces finely chopped white
  chocolate
½ cup heavy (whipping) cream, at
  room temperature
1 pound cream cheese, at room
  temperature
4 large eggs, separated, at room
  temperature
4 teaspoons vanilla extract
Dash of salt

Topping
6 ounces finely chopped white
  chocolate
¼ cup heavy (whipping) cream, at
  room temperature
2 tablespoons light crème de cacao

Make the crust:

1. Butter a 9″ × 3″ or 9½″ × 2″ springform pan. Combine graham cracker crumbs, butter, and sugar in a food processor fitted with a metal blade and process until well blended. Press mixture evenly and firmly over bottom and up two-thirds of the sides of the springform pan.

Make the filling:

2. Place a rack in the center and preheat oven to 300°F. In a double boiler over hot—not simmering—water, melt the white chocolate, stirring frequently. Gradually stir in the cream until the mixture is smooth. Remove the pan from the water and cool slightly.

3. Using an electric mixer set at medium speed, beat the cream cheese in a large bowl until smooth. Add egg yolks one at a time, blending well after each addition, stopping occasionally to scrape down the sides of the bowl and the beaters. Stir in the white chocolate, vanilla, and salt. Beat at medium speed for 2 minutes.

4. Using an electric mixer set at low speed, beat the egg whites in a grease-free medium bowl until foamy. Increase the speed to high and continue beating until soft peaks form. Fold the egg whites into the white chocolate mixture. Pour into the crust.

5. Place the pan on a baking sheet. Bake until the cake rises and the top jiggles slightly when shaken, about 55 minutes. Turn off the oven. Let cake stand in the oven for 1 hour. (It will sink.) Transfer the cake in the pan to a wire rack and cool completely.

Make the topping:

6. In a double boiler over hot—not simmering—water, melt the white chocolate, stirring frequently. Gradually stir in the cream until the mixture is smooth. Stir in the crème de cacao. Pour the topping over the cooled cake. Refrigerate until the topping is set. Cover with plastic wrap and refrigerate at least 4 hours.

7. At least 2 hours before serving, remove the cake from the refrigerator and release the sides of the springform. Serve at room temperature.

Do ahead: The cheesecake can be made and refrigerated up to 3 days in advance. It can be frozen in the pan, tightly covered with plastic wrap and aluminum foil, for up to 1 month. Defrost the wrapped cake in the refrigerator overnight.

MAKES 10 TO 12 SERVINGS.

The creator: Marlene Sorosky,
author of numerous cookbooks,
syndicated columnist, and
Los Angeles radio show host

Torta del Frate

This cake possesses a professional, "pastry shop" appearance, despite its ease of preparation. It's hard to find a better example of a dessert that demonstrates the lovely marriage of white chocolate and hazelnuts.

Cake

8 ounces finely chopped white chocolate, melted and tepid

2 cups heavy (whipping) cream, at room temperature

1 cup toasted, skinned, and ground hazelnuts (see index)

6 tablespoons Frangelico

1 8-inch round genoise (see index)

¼ cup water

Garnish

2 to 3 ounces white chocolate shavings (see index)

1 tablespoon unsweetened cocoa powder (preferably Dutch process)

1. In a large bowl, combine the melted white chocolate with the cream, ½ cup of the hazelnuts, and 2 tablespoons of Frangelico.

2. Using a long, serrated knife, slice the genoise horizontally into three equal layers. In a small bowl, combine the remaining Frangelico and

water. Place a cake layer, cut side up, on a serving platter. Brush with enough of the Frangelico mixture to moisten. Spread one-fourth of the white chocolate mixture over the cake layer. Top with the second cake layer and repeat the process using more Frangelico mixture and one-fourth of the filling. Top with the third layer, brush with enough Frangelico mixture to moisten, and spread the remaining cream to evenly cover the top and sides of the cake. Gently press the remaining hazelnuts on the sides of the cake.

    3.   Decorate the cake top with white chocolate shavings. Lightly sift the cocoa powder on top of the shavings. Refrigerate for at least 6 hours before serving.

Do ahead: The genoise can be made up to 1 day in advance, or frozen up to 1 month.

MAKES 8 TO 10 SERVINGS.

The creator: Nunzio Patruno, executive chef for The Monte Carlo Living Room in Philadelphia, Pennsylvania

5
Pies,
Pastries,
and
Breads

White Chocolate Pecan Pie

Rich, rich, rich is the way to describe this dessert; surprisingly, it is not overly sweet. White chocolate makes a classic pecan pie moister and creamier. This pie requires a longer cooking time than a more traditional version.

3 large eggs, at room temperature
⅔ cup sugar
5 tablespoons unsalted butter, melted
½ cup light corn syrup
½ cup dark corn syrup
1½ cups pecans
4 ounces coarsely chopped white
    chocolate
1 unbaked 9-inch pie crust (see
    index)

1. Position a rack in the lower third and preheat oven to 350°F. Using an electric mixer set at medium speed, beat the eggs in a large bowl until pale yellow and a thick ribbon forms when the beaters are lifted. Add the sugar and beat until thick and creamy. Add the butter and light and dark corn syrups and mix to blend. Stir in 1 cup of the pecans and the white chocolate.

2. Pour the mixture into the pie crust and top the pie decoratively with the remaining pecans. Cover loosely with aluminum foil. Bake for 15 minutes, remove the foil, and continue baking until a cake tester inserted in

76

the center of the pie comes out clean, about 1 hour. Transfer the pie in the pan to a wire rack and cool completely.

Do ahead: The pie can be made and refrigerated up to 1 day in advance. Serve at room temperature or reheated.

MAKES 8 SERVINGS.

*The creator: Laura Davidian, chef
of Georgie's Bar and Grill in
Encino, California*

White Chocolate–Hazelnut Tartlets

◈

White chocolate and hazelnut may be one of the more ubiquitous combinations—but that's because the ingredients work so well together. The dough may break a bit while you're working with it, but it's easy to patch.

Tartlets

¾ pound unsalted butter, at room
    temperature
1 cup sugar
1 large egg yolk, at room
    temperature
3 to 3½ cups flour
4 tablespoons finely chopped toasted
    hazelnuts (see index)

Filling

1½ teaspoons unflavored gelatin
⅓ cup Frangelico
4 tablespoons sugar
3 large eggs, separated, at room
    temperature
1 tablespoon cornstarch
¾ cup milk
6 ounces finely chopped white
    chocolate, melted and tepid
1 tablespoon white crème de cacao

2 tablespoons finely chopped toasted
*   hazelnuts (see index)*
1 cup heavy (whipping) cream,
*   whipped and chilled*

Garnish
Fresh raspberries or finely chopped
*   toasted hazelnuts*

Make the tartlets:
    1.   Position a rack in the center and preheat oven to 375°F. Using an electric mixer set at medium speed, cream the butter and sugar in a medium bowl until light and fluffy. Beat in the egg yolk. Mix in by hand just enough of the flour, ½ cup at a time, to form a dough that can be rolled. Mix in the hazelnuts. Divide the dough into twelve equal pieces and roll each into a 6-inch round. Store half of the dough in the refrigerator until it's time to work with it. (Note: If making the tarts on a warm day, the pastry may become oily. Immediately wrap in plastic and chill for 1 hour in the refrigerator before rolling out.)

    2.   Place the dough in twelve ungreased 4-inch-diameter, ¾-inch-deep tartlet pans and press gently to adhere to sides and bottoms. Trim edges. Patch any holes with small pieces of dough. Using a fork, prick the pastry on the bottom of the pans several times. Bake for about 10 minutes, or until the pastry begins to brown. (If edges of pastry brown too quickly, cover loosely with foil.) Transfer tartlets in the pans to a wire rack to cool completely. Remove the tartlets from the pans.

Make the filling:
    3.   In a small bowl, soften the gelatin in the Frangelico. Cover and set aside. Using an electric mixer set at medium speed, beat the egg yolks with the sugar in a large bowl until pale yellow and a ribbon forms when the beaters are lifted.

    4.   In a small bowl, combine the cornstarch with 2 tablespoons of

the milk to form a thin paste. Blend into the egg yolk mixture. In a heavy medium saucepan over medium heat, scald the remaining milk. (Do not boil.) Gradually whisk the milk into the egg yolk mixture. Return the mixture to the saucepan. Reduce the heat to low and cook until thickened, stirring constantly; do not boil. Stir in the gelatin mixture, melted white chocolate, crème de cacao, and chopped hazelnuts. Stir until smooth. Set aside to cool completely. (Note: The custard will be slightly thick at this point.)

5.   Using an electric mixer set at low speed, beat the egg whites in a grease-free large bowl until they start to foam. Gradually increase the speed to high and continue beating until the egg whites form stiff peaks. Fold egg whites gently into the custard. Fold in the chilled whipped cream. Fill the tartlets with custard and refrigerate, loosely covered, until set, about 1 hour. Garnish each tartlet with fresh raspberries or hazelnuts, if desired.

Do ahead: The tartlets can be made and refrigerated up to 1 day in advance. Garnish just before serving.

MAKES 12 SERVINGS.

The creator: Megan Timothy,
chef/proprietor of La Maida House,
a bed-and-breakfast establishment in
North Hollywood, California

At right: White Chocolate Mousse to Go
On following page: White Chocolate Coeur à la Crème

White Chocolate Cannoli

This Sicilian pastry was once wrapped around bamboo cane (called canna) to achieve its shape. Today, you can create the same effect with the easier-to-obtain cannoli forms, available at most cookware shops. In this recipe, white chocolate adds textural contrast to the creamy filling and enhances the richness of the ricotta cheese.

Filling

1 pound ricotta cheese
⅔ cup confectioners' sugar
Zest from ½ large orange (approx. ½ teaspoon)
½ cup pistachio nuts, toasted (see index)
⅓ cup white chocolate chips

Shells

1 cup flour
Pinch of salt
1 teaspoon baking powder
1 teaspoon confectioners' sugar
1 tablespoon unsalted butter, at room temperature
1 large egg, at room temperature
1 teaspoon vanilla extract
About ½ cup flat beer
Peanut oil, for frying

Garnish (optional)

6 ounces finely chopped white chocolate, melted
½ cup finely chopped toasted pistachio nuts (see index)

Make the filling:

1.   In a food processor fitted with a metal blade, blend the cheese, confectioners' sugar, and zest until smooth. Transfer to a medium bowl; fold in the pistachio nuts and white chocolate chips. Cover and refrigerate until chilled and slightly thickened, at least 1 hour.

Make the shells:

2.   In a food processor fitted with a metal blade, blend the flour, salt, baking powder, confectioners' sugar, butter, egg, and vanilla. With the machine running, add just enough of the beer to make a dough that begins to pull away from the sides of the bowl and form a solid mass. Remove the dough from the processor, wrap tightly in plastic wrap, and let rest at room temperature for 1 hour.

Assemble:

3.   On a flat, clean surface, roll the dough to a 12″ × 12″ square between two sheets of plastic wrap. Cut into nine 4-inch squares. Wrap the dough around cannoli forms and seal the ends together carefully with a little water. Add enough oil to come three inches up the sides of a deep frying pan and heat to 350°F. Carefully place three cannoli shells at a time into the hot oil. Hold the cannoli down with the back of a metal spatula or turn them over, if possible, to brown evenly on both sides, about 3 minutes. Transfer to paper towels to drain and cool slightly. Repeat the process with the remaining dough.

4.   Remove the cannoli forms while still warm to the touch by holding a shell with one hand and carefully pulling the form out with the other. Dip the ends of the shells in melted white chocolate and chopped pistachio nuts, if desired. Allow to cool and harden completely before filling.

5.   Bring the filling to room temperature and spoon into a pastry bag without a tip. Pipe an equal amount of filling into each of the nine shells. Serve immediately.

Do ahead: The cannoli shells can be made and stored in an airtight container up to 8 hours in advance. The filling can be made and refrigerated up to 8 hours in advance.

MAKES 9 SERVINGS.

The creator: Joyce Resnik, recipe tester for Bon Appétit *magazine and food writer*

Petits Pains

These petits pains are quick and easy to make, thanks to packaged puff pastry which can be purchased from most supermarkets. You can make them solely with white chocolate—simply eliminate the bittersweet. A deliciously different variation is to make the petit pains with Nestlé® Alpine White™ with Almonds bars. If you prepare these in advance, be sure to reheat them before serving.

1 17½-ounce package frozen puff
    pastry sheets, defrosted
3 3-ounce white chocolate bars
3 1.45-ounce bittersweet or
    semisweet chocolate bars
¼ cup cold water
1 large egg, beaten to blend

1.   Line two baking sheets with parchment paper.
2.   Place one sheet of puff pastry on a lightly floured surface. Roll it into a 12″ × 12″ square. Using a sharp knife, cut the square into three equal strips. Cut each strip into three equal squares, to total nine squares.
3.   Using a small, sharp knife, cut each of the white chocolate bars along the scored lines to make six equal pieces from each bar, or 18 total. (It does not matter if they break unevenly, as they will melt while baking.) Using a small, sharp knife, cut each of the dark chocolate bars along the scored lines to make 12 equal pieces from each bar, or 36 total.
4.   Lightly brush the chocolate pieces with cold water. Place a piece of white chocolate on the edge of each pastry square. Arrange two pieces of

dark chocolate on top of the white chocolate. Roll the dough into cylinders. Place the cylinders seam side down and two inches apart on the prepared baking sheets. Repeat rolling and filling procedure with the second sheet of puff pastry. Allow the cylinders to rest at room temperature for 1 hour before baking.

5.   Position a rack in the center and preheat oven to 400°F. Lightly brush the petits pains with the beaten egg. Let stand 10 minutes. Brush the petits pains with the egg mixture again. Lightly score tops with the tines of a fork, being careful not to pierce the dough.

6.   Bake until the petits pains have risen and are golden brown, about 15 to 20 minutes. Remove from oven and transfer to a wire rack to cool for about 15 minutes before serving. Cover and store at room temperature.

Do ahead: The petits pains can be made up to 3 days in advance and frozen for up to 2 months.

MAKES 18 SERVINGS.

The creator: Bess Greenstone,
Los Angeles–based recipe developer
and writer

Papaya, Macadamia Nut, and White Chocolate Strudel

This Hawaiian-inspired recipe must be made with ripe, sweet papayas.

¼ cup flour
¼ cup packed light brown sugar
½ teaspoon ground nutmeg
8 sheets filo dough
8 tablespoons unsalted butter, melted
2 very ripe, sweet papayas, peeled
    and cut into ¼-inch slices
¾ cup chopped macadamia nuts
¾ cup chopped white chocolate

1.   Position a rack in the center and preheat oven to 350°F. Lightly butter a baking sheet.

2.   In a small bowl, combine the flour, brown sugar, and nutmeg.

3.   Place 1 sheet of filo on a heavy large baking sheet. Top with a second sheet and brush with melted butter. Continue to layer with 2 sheets of filo at a time, brushing the top with melted butter until all the sheets are used. Place papaya slices starting ½-inch from the border of one long side of the filo stack. Leave ½-inch borders on the two short sides. Sprinkle the flour mixture over the papaya. Sprinkle the nuts and white chocolate over the flour mixture.

4.   Starting at the filled edge, roll the filo into a log shape and place

seam side down on the prepared baking sheet. Seal ends closed using melted butter, if necessary. Lightly brush melted butter over the top of the log. Bake until golden brown, about 30 minutes. Transfer the log to a wire rack and cool completely. Using a serrated knife, cut the strudel into 1-inch-wide slices.

Do ahead: The strudel can be made, wrapped airtight, and stored at room temperature up to 1 day in advance.

MAKES 12 SERVINGS.

The creator: KT Burdon, an East Hampton, New York, caterer

White Satin Tart

Here's an easy-to-make dessert that looks as good as it tastes.

Crust
1 cup flour
Dash of salt
*8 tablespoons unsalted butter, cut
    into ½-inch pieces, chilled*
*3 ounces cream cheese, cut into
    ½-inch pieces, chilled*

Filling
1 cup fresh raspberries
1 tablespoon sugar
1 teaspoon cornstarch
*4 ounces finely chopped white
    chocolate*
*8 tablespoons unsalted butter, at
    room temperature*
⅓ cup superfine sugar
2 large eggs, at room temperature

Decoration
*2 ounces coarsely chopped semisweet
    chocolate*
1 teaspoon unsalted butter
1 teaspoon vegetable oil

Make the crust:

1. In a food processor fitted with a metal blade, combine the flour and salt. Distribute the butter and cream cheese evenly over the flour and process using on–off pulses until the dough just starts to come together; do not overwork. Form the dough into a ball. Wrap it in plastic wrap and refrigerate for 30 to 40 minutes.

2. On a lightly floured surface, roll the dough out to fit a 10-inch tart pan. (If the dough tears, patch it with scraps.) Trim the edges of the dough. Freeze for 1 hour.

3. Position a rack in the center and preheat oven to 350°F. Line the crust with a piece of foil and fill it with pie weights or beans. Bake for 10 minutes, remove the weights and the foil, and continue to bake until uniformly golden, about 10 minutes. Transfer the crust in the pan to a wire rack and cool completely.

Make the filling:

4. Puree the raspberries in a blender or food processor and strain through a fine-mesh sieve. Add the sugar and cornstarch and stir until well combined.

5. In a heavy small saucepan over medium heat, bring the puree to a boil and cook until thickened, stirring frequently, about 3 minutes. Cool slightly and spread the puree over the baked crust.

6. In a double boiler, over hot—not simmering—water, melt the white chocolate, stirring frequently. Let cool until tepid.

7. Using an electric mixer set at medium speed, beat the butter in a large bowl until light and fluffy. Gradually add the sugar and continue beating until pale yellow. Mix in the tepid white chocolate.

8. Add 1 egg. Beat on high speed for 3 minutes. Add the other egg and beat for 3 minutes more.

9. Spoon the filling into the pie crust and smooth it evenly and carefully.

Decorate:

10. In a heavy small saucepan over very low heat, melt the

chocolate and the butter, stirring constantly. Add the oil and mix well. Cool slightly.

11.   Use either a parchment pastry bag with a very small hole snipped in the tip or a regular small pastry bag fitted with a #2 plain tip. Starting from the center of the tart and working outward, pipe a fine spiral of chocolate on top of the tart. Refrigerate the tart until the spiral is slightly set, about 7 minutes.

12.   Working from the center of the spiral to the outer edges, draw the blade of a small, sharp knife lightly through the chocolate spiral to create a spider web effect. To ensure a clear design, be sure to wipe the knife after each line. Refrigerate the tart for at least 4 hours before serving.

Do ahead: The tart can be made and refrigerated up to 2 days in advance.

MAKES 12 SERVINGS.

*The creator: Nanci Main,
pastry chef/co-owner of The Ark
restaurant in Nahcotta, Washington*

90

White Chocolate–Toasted Almond Stollen

~~~

A stollen is a traditional German Christmas bread that's served throughout the holiday season. In this successful variation, white chocolate is added to the toasted almond filling. Stollen remains fresh longer than most breads and tastes great when toasted and lightly buttered.

Filling

6 ounces finely chopped white
  chocolate
6 ounces ground toasted almonds
  (see index)
1 teaspoon almond extract

Stollen

1 package (½ ounce) dry yeast
⅔ cup warm beer
3½ cups flour
½ pound unsalted butter, at room
  temperature
½ cup sugar

1 large egg, at room temperature
2 teaspoons almond extract
½ teaspoon salt
1⅓ cups raisins
⅓ cup candied fruit
1 cup almonds, chopped
Milk

Garnish

Melted butter
Granulated sugar
Confectioners' sugar

Make the filling:

1. Melt the white chocolate in a double boiler over hot—not simmering—water, stirring frequently.

2. Blend the white chocolate, almonds, and almond extract in a food processor. Shape the mixture into two 10-inch-long rolls. Cover with plastic wrap and refrigerate.

Make the stollen:

3. In a small bowl, dissolve the yeast in warm beer. Stir in 1 cup of the flour. Cover with plastic, and let rise for about 1½ hours in a warm, draft-free area.

4. Using a heavy-duty mixer fitted with the paddle attachment, cream the butter and sugar together until light and fluffy. Beat in the egg, almond extract, and salt. Beat the yeast mixture into the egg mixture. Replace the paddle with the dough hook. Mix in 2 cups of the flour. Knead dough at medium speed until dough is just slightly sticky to the touch, about 4 minutes.

5. Combine remaining ½ cup flour with raisins, candied fruit, and nuts. Add to the dough and knead until smooth and elastic.

6. Transfer the dough to a large bowl, cover with plastic, and let rise in a warm, draft-free area until doubled in volume, about 1 hour. Punch the dough down. Roll the dough on a lightly floured surface into a 12″ × 12″ square.

7. Place the two rolls of chocolate mixture parallel to each other about two inches from the top and bottom edges of the dough square. Fold dough over chocolate so that the edges meet in the middle, and seal the edges securely with milk. Transfer the dough to a large, heavy baking sheet.

8. Position a rack in the center and preheat oven to 350°F. Allow dough to rise in a warm, draft-free area for 45 minutes. Bake until golden brown and hollow-sounding when inverted and tapped on the bottom, about 45 minutes.

9. Transfer the stollen on the baking sheet to a wire rack and cool. When slightly cool, brush with melted butter and sugar, then cool completely. Sprinkle with confectioners' sugar. Store at room temperature, wrapped airtight.

Do ahead: The stollen can be made up to 5 days in advance.

MAKES 1 STOLLEN.

The creator: Nigel Richardson,
chef for The Fort restaurant
in Denver, Colorado

White Chocolate Cinnamon Bread

This bread has all the classic virtues of a fresh-baked cinnamon loaf—its aroma will swirl through your kitchen. The perky, crisp taste of cinnamon seems to balance the richness of white chocolate for a dynamic flavor duo. Don't forget to try a slice or two toasted.

Bread
6½ to 7 cups bread flour
6 tablespoons sugar
2 tablespoons dry yeast
1½ teaspoons salt
1 cup milk
¾ cup water
⅓ cup unsalted butter, at room
  temperature
3 large eggs, at room temperature
½ cup sugar
2 teaspoons ground cinnamon
1 pound coarsely chopped white
  chocolate

Streusel
⅓ cup flour
⅓ cup packed light brown sugar
1 teaspoon ground cinnamon

3 tablespoons unsalted butter, at
room temperature
1 large egg white, lightly beaten

Make the bread:

1.   Using an electric mixer set at medium speed, blend 2 cups of the flour, sugar, yeast, and salt in a large bowl. In a heavy medium saucepan over low heat, combine milk, water, and butter until the mixture registers between 120°F to 125°F on a candy thermometer. Gradually add milk mixture to the flour mixture and beat at medium speed until smooth for about 2 minutes, scraping the bowl occasionally.

2.   Beat in the eggs and ½ cup flour. Increase the speed to high and continue beating 2 minutes, scraping the bowl occasionally. Using an electric mixer fitted with the paddle attachment, knead in enough additional flour to make a stiff dough. Turn out on lightly floured board; knead until smooth and elastic. Place in a lightly buttered bowl, turn the dough over to butter the top side, and cover with plastic wrap. Let rise in a warm, draft-free area until doubled in volume, about 1 hour.

3.   Meanwhile, in a medium bowl, combine the sugar and cinnamon. Lightly butter the bottom and sides of two 9″ × 5″ × 3″ loaf pans. Line the bottoms of the pans with parchment paper. Dust the bottom and sides with flour; tap out the excess.

4.   Punch the dough down; divide in half. Roll each half into a 9″ × 14″ rectangle. Sprinkle an equal amount of the cinnamon–sugar mixture on each rectangle. Place the chocolate pieces randomly over each rectangle. Beginning at the short end, tightly roll dough as for a jelly roll and tuck the ends under. Place in the prepared pans. Cover loosely with plastic wrap and let rise in warm, draft-free area until doubled in bulk, about 45 minutes to 1 hour. Preheat the oven to 350°F.

Make the streusel:

5.   In a small bowl, combine the flour, sugar, and cinnamon. Using

two knives, cut in the softened butter until it resembles coarse meal. Brush the loaves with the egg white. Pat an equal amount of streusel onto each loaf. Loosely tent each loaf with aluminum foil and bake 45 minutes. Remove the foil tents; bake 5 minutes longer, or until golden. Transfer to wire racks and cool completely. Store at room temperature, wrapped airtight.

Do ahead: The bread can be made up to 2 days in advance.

MAKES 2 LARGE LOAVES.

The creator: Joyce Resnik, recipe tester for Bon Appétit *magazine and food writer*

At right: Blonde Bombshell
On following page: Riesling-Poached Pears with White Chocolate Ganache

6
A Hint of White Chocolate

Tri-Chocolate Terrine

It's easy to make this sophisticated dessert for a dinner party; if you like, you can divide the work between three days. It's rich enough to be served on its own, but you can surround each slice with crème Anglaise and garnish the plate with raspberries.

Dark chocolate layer

3 ounces finely chopped bittersweet
  or semisweet chocolate
1 tablespoon dark rum
2 large eggs
½ large egg yolk
2 tablespoons sugar
1 cup heavy (whipping) cream,
  chilled

Milk chocolate layer

4 ounces finely chopped milk
  chocolate
1 tablespoon light rum

2 large eggs
½ large egg yolk
2 tablespoons sugar
1 cup heavy (whipping) cream,
  chilled

White chocolate layer

4 ounces finely chopped white
  chocolate
1 tablespoon white rum
2 large eggs
½ large egg yolk
2 tablespoons sugar
1 cup heavy (whipping) cream,
  chilled

Make the dark chocolate layer:

1. Line a 12″ × 4″ terrine mold with enough parchment paper to overhang edges on each of the long sides by 2 inches.

2. In a double boiler over hot—not simmering—water, melt the chocolate with the rum and stir together into a paste. Set aside to cool to room temperature.

3. Using an electric mixer set at medium speed, beat the eggs, egg

yolk, and sugar in a medium bowl until blended. Increase the speed to high and beat in the chocolate paste until smooth, about 3 minutes. Cover and refrigerate.

4. Using an electric mixer, whip the cream in a bowl set over a larger bowl filled with ice until the cream forms a slowly dissolving ribbon when dropped from the beaters. Remove the bowl from the ice.

5. Place the bowl with the chocolate mixture over the bowl filled with ice. Using a wooden spoon, stir in one-fourth of the whipped cream until the mixture is smooth and no streaks remain. Fold in the remaining cream.

6. Pour the mixture evenly into the terrine mold, cover the mold with plastic wrap, and freeze until firm, at least 2 hours or overnight.

Make the milk chocolate layer:

7. Repeat Steps 2 through 6. Pour the milk chocolate mixture on top of the frozen dark chocolate layer. Freeze until firm, at least 2 hours or overnight.

Make the white chocolate layer:

8. Repeat Steps 2 through 6. Pour the white chocolate mixture on top of the frozen milk chocolate layer. Freeze until very firm, at least 6 hours or overnight. To serve, invert mold onto serving platter, and using a serrated knife, cut the terrine into 1-inch slices.

Do ahead: The terrine can be made and frozen up to 1 week in advance.

MAKES 12 SERVINGS.

The creator: Salomon Montezinos,
chef/owner of Deja-Vu restaurant
in Philadelphia, Pennsylvania

Riesling-Poached Pears
with White Chocolate Ganache

❧

The pears are delicately poached in Riesling and then coated with a smooth white chocolate ganache. It's an easy, elegant fruit dessert that's also visually appealing.

Pears
1 bottle Riesling wine (750 milliliters)
2 cups sugar
4 whole cloves
2 bay leaves
1 vanilla bean
6 whole, ripe Bartlett pears

Ganache
1 cup heavy (whipping) cream
10 ounces finely chopped white chocolate

Garnish
6 mint sprigs

Poach the pears:
1.   In a heavy large saucepan over medium heat, bring the Riesling to a simmer with the sugar, cloves, bay leaves, and vanilla bean.

2.   Using a sharp knife, peel the pears as smoothly as possible, leaving the stems on. Remove the entire core from the bottom side of the pears. Lower the pears into the simmering syrup (reduce the heat to low, if necessary) and poach until they are tender, about 20 minutes. Remove the pears from the liquid and set aside to cool.

3.   Strain the poaching liquid through a fine-mesh strainer and return to the saucepan. Boil over high heat until the syrup reaches 238°F on a candy thermometer. Cool completely. Set aside.

Make the ganache:

4.   In a saucepan over medium-high heat, bring the cream to a boil and remove from heat. Gradually whisk in the white chocolate until the mixture is smooth.

Assemble:

5.   Pat the pears dry with paper towels and cut a small portion off the bottom of each pear so it will stand upright. Place the pears upright in a shallow dish or pan and carefully ladle the ganache over each to achieve a smooth coating. Remove to a serving plate and carefully coat again to achieve an even coating. A small amount of ganache will rest in a circle around each pear. Allow the pears to cool completely.

6.   Place each pear on a dessert plate, spoon some of the poaching syrup around it, and garnish with a mint sprig.

MAKES 6 SERVINGS.

*The creator: Greg Higgins,
executive chef for the Heathman Hotel
in Portland, Oregon*

Filo-Wrapped Bananas

When I first read this recipe, I thought, "no way." Then I tasted the filo-wrapped bananas and was pleasantly surprised: they are actually quite delicious. Each mouthful brings you crispy filo, a soft, rich center, and the crunch of almonds. They're a great breakfast or brunch pastry and a contender for outstanding comfort food. The recipe may be increased proportionally, as desired.

> *2 sheets filo dough*
> *1 very ripe large banana*
> *2 tablespoons grated white chocolate*
> *2 tablespoons slivered, blanched*
>   *almonds, lightly toasted (see*
>   *index)*
> *Vegetable oil*
> *Confectioners' sugar, for garnish*

1. Fold 1 sheet of filo dough lengthwise in half. Cut the banana widthwise in half. Position a banana half on one short end of the filo dough.
2. Sprinkle 1 tablespoon of the white chocolate over the banana. Sprinkle 1 tablespoon of the almonds over the white chocolate. Roll the filo dough over the banana and continue to roll to half of the length of the dough. Fold over the sides of the filo dough, moisten the opposite end with water, and continue rolling the dough to the end. Seal the edges carefully. Repeat with the second filo sheet and the remaining banana half.

3. In a heavy deep skillet, add enough vegetable oil to come two inches up the sides of the pan. Heat the oil to 350°F. Carefully lower the bananas seam side down into the oil and cook, watching carefully, until both sides are golden brown. Using a slotted spoon, remove the bananas to paper towels to drain. Sprinkle with confectioners' sugar. Serve immediately.

MAKES 2 SERVINGS.

The creator: KT Burdon, an East Hampton, New York, caterer

Black Mission Fig Ravioli with White Chocolate Sauce

The slightly sweet "raviolis" are more like a crisp pastry shell. The intensity of the fruity, dark chocolate filling—which tastes a little like warm chocolate pudding—is matched by an equally bold white chocolate sauce. You can make the raviolis in the morning and cover and refrigerate them until you are ready to fry them. You will need a pasta machine to make this recipe successfully.

Fig filling
1½ cups white port
20 dried Black Mission figs
8 ounces finely chopped semisweet
   chocolate

Sauce
1 large egg yolk, at room
   temperature
1½ tablespoons sugar
4 ounces finely chopped white
   chocolate, melted and tepid
4 tablespoons unsalted butter, melted
½ cup crème fraîche (see index)
½ cup heavy (whipping) cream

Ravioli
2 cups flour
1 large egg, at room temperature

¼ cup sugar
¼ cup water
1 egg yolk
1 tablespoon milk
Vegetable oil, for frying
Figs, for garnish

Make the filling:

1.   In a heavy small saucepan over high heat, boil the port until it reduces to ¾ cup. Cut the figs in half, remove pulp, and add pulp to the reduced port. In a double boiler over hot—not simmering—water, melt the chocolate, stirring frequently. Stir the chocolate into the port. Spoon into a pastry bag without a tip and refrigerate.

Make the sauce:

2.   In a double boiler over simmering water, whisk the egg yolk and sugar together until the sugar is dissolved. Transfer to a medium bowl. Using an electric mixer set at low speed, blend the chocolate into the egg yolk mixture. Mix in the melted butter. Beat in the crème fraîche and heavy cream until smooth and creamy. Cover and refrigerate.

Make the raviolis:

4.   In a food processor fitted with a metal blade, combine the flour, egg, sugar, and only as much of the ¼ cup of water as needed to bind the dough. Process until the dough pulls away from the sides of the bowl. Cover and refrigerate for 20 minutes before rolling.

5.   Cut the dough into four pieces. Flatten one piece of the dough (keep remainder covered), then fold in thirds. Turn the pasta machine to the widest setting and run the dough through several times until smooth and velvety, folding before each run and dusting with flour if sticky. (The number of runs will depend on how vigorously the dough was kneaded by hand.) Adjust the machine to the next widest setting. Run the dough through the machine without folding. Repeat, narrowing rollers after each

run, dusting with flour as necessary, until pasta is $\frac{1}{16}$-inch thick.

6. In a small bowl, combine the egg yolk and milk and brush over the rolled sheets of dough. On two of the rolled sheets, drop 1 heaping teaspoon of the fig filling in 12 evenly spaced mounds. Cover each sheet with a second sheet of dough and cut with a sharp knife or fluted pastry wheel into approximately $1\frac{1}{2}$-inch squares. Seal edges tightly by pressing dough together with fingers.

7. Into a heavy deep frying pan, pour enough oil to come 2 inches up the sides of the pan. Heat oil to 375°F. Carefully lower a few raviolis at a time into the oil and fry until golden brown, about $1\frac{1}{2}$ minutes per side. Remove from the oil using a slotted spoon and drain on paper towels.

Serve:

8. Spoon about 2 tablespoons white chocolate sauce on each plate. Top sauce with three raviolis and garnish each plate with a fresh fig, cut into quarters. Serve immediately.

Do ahead: The raviolis can be made through Step 6 and refrigerated stored in a single layer, covered loosely, up to 8 hours or overnight. The sauce can be made up to 2 days in advance.

MAKES 3 DOZEN, OR 8 SERVINGS.

The Creator: Peter Rosenberg,
executive chef for the Hotel Bel-Air
in Bel Air, California

White Chocolate Fondue

You'll be surprised how well the delicate flavor of white chocolate lends itself to pairings with a wide variety of fruit. This light, refreshing dessert is quick to assemble and ideal for summer entertaining, particularly if it's impromptu. For a variation, substitute plain white chocolate for the Nestlé® Alpine White™ with Almonds and a fruit-flavored liqueur of your choice for the amaretto.

1 pint strawberries, with stems
5 apricots, pitted and quartered
1 banana, sliced thickly
3 kiwi fruits, peeled and quartered
Mint leaves, for garnish
1-pound pound cake, cubed
   (optional)

10 ounces finely chopped Nestlé®
   Alpine White™ with Almonds
6 tablespoons heavy (whipping)
   cream
2 teaspoons amaretto

1.   Arrange the fruit attractively on one dessert platter. Garnish with fresh mint leaves. Arrange the pound cake on a separate platter, if desired.

2.   In a double boiler over hot—not simmering—water, melt the white chocolate with the cream, stirring frequently. Stir in the amaretto. Transfer to a heat-proof bowl and place on a warming tray set at low temperature in the center of the dining table. Serve with the fruit platter. Present fondue skewers or long forks for dipping. (Or, melt the white chocolate with the cream in a fondue pot and serve in the pot.)

MAKES 6 SERVINGS.

Black Satin Fudge Cake with White Chocolate Crème Anglaise

The cake is ultra-moist and fudgy. When served warm in a pool of cool white chocolate crème Anglaise, it's transformed into a stellar dessert worth aerobicizing an extra hour for.

Crème Anglaise
7 large egg yolks, at room
    temperature
2 tablespoons sugar
1 teaspoon cornstarch
2¼ cups milk
6 ounces finely chopped white
    chocolate
2 tablespoons white crème de cacao

Cake
½ pound unsalted butter, at room
    temperature

8 ounces finely chopped unsweetened
    chocolate
4 ounces finely chopped semisweet
    chocolate
1 cup sugar
⅓ cup light corn syrup
5 large eggs, at room temperature
2 teaspoons vanilla extract
Pinch of salt

Garnish (optional)
1 pint fresh berries

Make the crème Anglaise:
  1.   Using an electric mixer set at medium speed, beat the egg yolks with the sugar in a large bowl until a thin ribbon forms when the beaters are lifted, about 3 to 4 minutes. Beat in the cornstarch.
  2.   In a heavy large saucepan over medium-high heat, heat the milk until hot. Remove the pan from the heat and stir in the white chocolate,

blending until smooth. Gradually stir 1½ cups of the white chocolate mixture into the egg yolk mixture until blended. Pour this mixture back into the saucepan. Continue cooking over medium-low heat, stirring constantly with a wooden spoon, until the custard has thickened slightly and leaves a path across the back of the spoon when you run your finger down it, about 2 to 4 minutes. Do not let the custard come to a boil. Remove the pan from the heat and immediately strain the custard through a fine-mesh sieve into a non-aluminum bowl.

3. Set the bowl over a larger bowl filled with ice water. Stir the custard frequently until chilled, about 10 to 15 minutes. Remove the bowl from the ice water and stir in the crème de cacao. Cover and refrigerate.

Make the cake:

4. Position a rack in the center and preheat oven to 350°F. Lightly butter the bottom and sides of a 9-inch springform pan. Line the bottom of the pan with parchment paper. Dust the bottom and sides with flour; tap out the excess. Securely wrap the outside of the pan with heavy-duty aluminum foil to keep the batter from seeping out as it bakes.

5. In a heavy medium saucepan over very low heat, melt the butter and chocolates, stirring constantly. Remove from heat and let the mixture cool until tepid, about 5 to 10 minutes.

6. In a heavy medium saucepan over medium heat, combine ½ cup sugar and the corn syrup, stirring frequently until the mixture comes to a full boil. Using a heavy-duty electric mixer set at medium-high speed, beat the eggs with the remaining ½ cup sugar, vanilla, and salt in a large bowl until mixture triples in volume and forms a thick, pale yellow ribbon when the beaters are lifted, about 8 to 10 minutes.

7. Transfer the sugar syrup to a heat-proof measuring cup. Reduce the mixer speed to medium and slowly add the syrup to the egg mixture in a thin, steady stream. Reduce the speed to low and blend the chocolate mixture into the batter until incorporated. Scrape the batter into the prepared pan and smooth the top with a spatula.

8. Place the springform pan in a shallow roasting pan filled with

one inch of hot water. Place the roasting pan in the preheated oven and bake until a cake tester inserted into the center of the cake comes out clean, about 40 to 45 minutes. The cake will not spring back when gently pressed. Do not overbake the cake as it will firm up as it cools. Transfer the cake in the pan to a wire rack and let cool for 30 minutes. Invert the cake onto a large serving platter and carefully peel off the paper.

Assemble:

9. Spoon about 3 tablespoons of the crème Anglaise onto the center of each dessert plate. Place a slice of the warm cake in the center of the sauce. Garnish the plates with berries, if desired.

Do ahead: The cake can be made in advance and frozen up to 1 month; reheat before serving. (Bring to room temperature and warm, wrapped in aluminum foil, in a 350°F oven.) The crème Anglaise can be made and refrigerated up to 2 days in advance.

MAKES 10 SERVINGS.

The creator: Marlene Sorosky, author of numerous cookbooks, syndicated columnist, and Los Angeles radio show host

Mock Hostess Cupcakes

These ultra-moist, dark chocolate mini-cupcakes are filled with creamy white chocolate ganache. They're a variation on a whimsical cupcake that Michael Roberts serves at Los Angeles's Trumps restaurant at teatime.

Cupcakes
½ cup plus 2 tablespoons flour
2½ tablespoons cocoa powder
  (preferably Dutch process)
¾ teaspoon baking soda
¼ teaspoon salt
½ cup sugar
½ cup water
3 tablespoons vegetable oil
1½ teaspoons distilled white vinegar
1 teaspoon vanilla extract

Filling
1 cup heavy (whipping) cream
6 ounces finely chopped white
  chocolate

Glaze
3 ounces finely chopped bittersweet
  chocolate
3 tablespoons boiling water

Icing
1 tablespoon egg white, at room
  temperature
Pinch of cream of tartar
½ cup plus 2 to 3 tablespoons
  confectioners' sugar

Make the cupcakes:

1.   Position a rack in the center and preheat oven to 325°F. Lightly butter twenty-four 1¾″ × ¾″ (1 ounce) muffin or biscuit cups.

2.   Into a medium bowl, sift together the flour, cocoa, baking soda,

and salt. Mix in the sugar. Make a well in the center. Whisk in the water, oil, vinegar, and vanilla. Blend until smooth. (The batter will be very thin.)

3.   Spoon the batter into the prepared cups. Bake until a cake tester inserted into the center of one of the cupcakes comes out clean, about 12 to 14 minutes. Cool the cupcakes in the pans on a wire rack for 5 minutes. Remove the cupcakes from the pans and finish cooling on the rack.

Make the filling:

4.   In a heavy medium saucepan over medium-high heat, bring the cream to a boil. Add the white chocolate and remove from heat. Let the mixture stand briefly; stir until smooth. Transfer to a metal bowl and refrigerate until chilled thoroughly, stirring occasionally. (To speed the process, set the metal bowl over a larger bowl of ice water; stir the chocolate mixture until cool.) With an electric mixer, beat the white chocolate mixture just until fluffy, about 1 minute.

5.   Transfer the filling to a pastry bag fitted with a ⅜-inch plain tip. Insert the pastry tip ¼-inch into the bottom of each cupcake and squeeze a little filling into each one.

Make the glaze:

6.   Place the chocolate in a small bowl. Whisk in the boiling water and blend until smooth. One at a time, dip the top of each cupcake into the warm glaze. Turn the glazed cupcakes right side up and set them on a wire rack on top of a baking sheet. Refrigerate the cupcakes for 5 minutes to set the glaze.

Make the icing:

7.   In a medium bowl, whisk the egg white until frothy. Stir in the cream of tartar. Gradually mix in enough of the confectioners' sugar to make a fairly stiff and smooth icing. Fill a small paper cone with the icing and cut a ¹⁄₁₆-inch opening at the tip. Remove the cupcakes from the refrigerator. Pipe a design (a squiggle, spiral, etc.) on the top of each cupcake. Let the design harden and then cover and refrigerate the cupcakes. Serve at room temperature.

Do ahead: The cupcakes can be made and refrigerated up to 2 days in advance, or frozen up to 2 weeks.

MAKES 22 TO 24 MINIATURE CUPCAKES.

Black and White Soufflé

The semisweet chocolate flavor may be intense, but it doesn't overpower the white chocolate. This half-and-half soufflé is not only great looking, it's downright sexy.

Soufflé
3 tablespoons milk
¼ cup plus 1 tablespoon sugar
2 large egg yolks, at room temperature
3 large egg whites, at room temperature
½ teaspoon lemon juice
2 ounces finely chopped white chocolate, melted and tepid
2 ounces finely chopped semisweet chocolate, melted and tepid

Whipped cream
½ cup heavy (whipping) cream, chilled
½ teaspoon vanilla extract

Garnish
Confectioners' sugar

Make the soufflé:

1.   Position a rack in the center and preheat oven to 350° F. Butter a 6-inch diameter soufflé mold and sprinkle sugar on the bottom and sides. Discard excess sugar. Wrap a 6″ × 4″ piece of cardboard in aluminum foil.

2.   In a heavy small saucepan over medium heat, combine the milk and ¼ cup of the sugar, stirring constantly to dissolve the sugar. Remove from heat and whisk in the egg yolks; divide the mixture into two medium bowls and set aside.

3.   Using an electric mixer set at low speed, beat the egg whites with the lemon juice in a grease-free medium bowl until they start to foam. Gradually increase the speed to high and continue beating the egg whites

until they form soft peaks. Gradually beat in the remaining sugar and continue beating the egg whites until they form stiff peaks.

4. Using an electric mixer, beat the white chocolate into one bowl of the milk mixture until smooth. Using an electric mixer with clean beaters, beat the semisweet chocolate into the other bowl of the milk mixture until smooth. Gently fold half the beaten egg whites into the white chocolate mixture. With a clean spatula, gently fold the remaining half of the beaten egg whites into the dark chocolate mixture.

5. Stand the prepared cardboard in the center of the prepared soufflé dish. Gently spoon the white mixture into one side of the dish, and the dark mixture into the other. Carefully lift the cardboard up and out and bake until the soufflé is puffed and the tops are firm and shake only slightly when the oven rack is gently moved, about 18 to 20 minutes. Do not open the oven door until the soufflé is done. Transfer the soufflé in the dish to a wire rack.

Make the whipped cream:

6. In a chilled bowl, beat the cream with the vanilla until it forms soft peaks.

Assemble:

7. Sprinkle the soufflé with confectioners' sugar. Immediately spoon an equal amount of soufflé—including both white and dark portions—onto two or three dessert plates. Serve the whipped cream, separately, in a bowl.

MAKES 2 TO 3 SERVINGS.

The creator: Margaret S. Fox,
chef/owner of Cafe Beaujolais
in Mendocino, California

Mocha Profiteroles
with White Chocolate Chip Cream

〰️

White chocolate chips add a little flavor and crunch to this charming dessert.

Profiteroles
2 cups water
2 ounces finely chopped semisweet chocolate
1 tablespoon instant espresso coffee
1 tablespoon sugar
Pinch of salt
16 tablespoons unsalted butter

2 cups flour
7 large eggs, at room temperature

Filling
12 ounces white chocolate chips
2 cups heavy (whipping) cream, whipped and chilled

Make the profiteroles:
1. Position a rack in the lower third and preheat oven to 425°F. Lightly butter a baking sheet. In a large saucepan over high heat, bring the water to a boil. Whisk in the chocolate and the instant espresso until well dissolved. Whisk in the sugar and salt. Add the butter and let mixture continue to boil until the butter is melted. Remove from heat. Add the flour all at once. Stir well with a wooden spoon, and cook over high heat until the mixture begins to pull away from the bottom and sides of the pan, about 30 seconds.
2. Remove the pan from heat and let the mixture cool until tepid. Using an electric mixer set at low speed, beat in 6 eggs one at a time, beating well after each addition, until the mixture is smooth and shiny.

3.   Immediately transfer the mixture to a pastry bag fitted with a ¾-inch plain tip. Pipe mixture onto the prepared baking sheet in 10 large mounds, about 3 inches in diameter. Lightly beat the remaining egg and brush it over the top of the piped dough with a pastry brush.

4.   Bake for about 20 to 25 minutes without opening the oven door. Reduce the heat to 350°F and bake an additional 20 minutes. Turn the oven off. Transfer the baking sheet to a wire rack to cool. Using a serrated knife, cut off the top third of each profiterole and set aside. Return the profiteroles to the oven for 15 minutes to dry the insides. Transfer the profiteroles to the wire rack to cool completely.

Make the filling:

5.   In a medium bowl, fold the white chocolate chips into the whipped cream.

Assemble:

6.   Spoon an equal amount of white chocolate chip cream into each profiterole and replace the top. Serve immediately.

Do ahead: The unfilled profiteroles can be prepared several hours in advance, covered, and kept at room temperature. The cream filling can be prepared 2 hours in advance, covered, and refrigerated. Assemble just before serving.

MAKES 10 SERVINGS.

The creator: Bonnie S. Bailey, owner of The Highland Gourmet, Inc., a cooking school and catering and retail shop in Birmingham, Alabama

Clay's Chocolate Ice Cream with White Chocolate Truffles

Chocolate ice cream doesn't get much richer and smoother than this one: it tastes like a frozen ganache. The white chocolate truffles contribute color and textural contrast.

Ice cream

1 cup half-and-half
¾ cup sugar
6 large egg yolks, at room temperature
5 ounces finely chopped semisweet chocolate
1 ounce (1 square) finely chopped unsweetened chocolate
2 tablespoons unsalted butter, at room temperature
2 cups heavy (whipping) cream
1 teaspoon vanilla extract

Truffles

5 ounces finely chopped white chocolate
6 tablespoons plus 2 teaspoons heavy (whipping) cream
2 tablespoons plus 1½ teaspoons unsalted butter, at room temperature
¼ teaspoon kirsch

Make the ice cream:

1. In a heavy saucepan over medium heat, warm the half-and-half with the sugar until the sugar dissolves, stirring occasionally.

2. In a medium bowl, whisk the egg yolks just enough to blend, then whisk in some of the warm half-and-half. Return the egg yolk mixture to the pan and cook over low heat, stirring constantly, until the mixture

coats the back of a spoon and leaves a clear path when a finger is drawn across the spoon, about 10 minutes. Pour the mixture through a fine-mesh sieve into a small bowl.

3. In a double boiler over hot—not simmering—water, melt the semisweet and unsweetened chocolates with the butter, stirring occasionally. Remove the pan from the water. Whisk in the warmed custard, two tablespoons at a time. (Adding the custard gradually to the chocolate will prevent the ice cream from getting little grains of chocolate in it.) Gradually whisk in the cream. Add the vanilla; cover and chill.

Make the truffles:

4. In a double boiler over hot—not simmering—water, melt the white chocolate, cream, and butter, stirring occasionally. Add the kirsch and pour into a flat pan in about a ½-inch deep layer. Cover and freeze until firm. Using a teaspoon, scoop out quarter-teaspoonfuls of the truffle mixture and roll into rough truffle-shaped balls. Cover and freeze.

5. Freeze the ice cream in an ice cream maker according to the manufacturer's instructions. Transfer the ice cream to a container. Fold in the truffles. Cover and freeze.

Do ahead: The ice cream can be made up to 4 days in advance. The truffles can be made up to 1 day in advance.

MAKES ABOUT 1 QUART.

The creators: Lindsey Shere, pastry chef for Chez Panisse in Berkeley, California, with Clay Wollard

Dark Chocolate Cookies
with White Chocolate Chunks

These simple-to-make cookies are very chocolaty, yet the white chocolate is never overpowered. The two chocolates harmonize and the nuts add textural contrast.

½ pound unsalted butter, at room
    temperature
1¾ cups sugar
2 large eggs, at room temperature
1½ teaspoons vanilla extract
1 ounce (1 square) unsweetened
    chocolate, melted and tepid
¼ cup sour cream
¾ pound coarsely chopped white
    chocolate
2½ cups flour
1 cup unsweetened cocoa (preferably
    Dutch process)
½ teaspoon baking soda
½ teaspoon baking powder
½ teaspoon salt
1 cup coarsely chopped Brazil nuts,
    pecans, or walnuts

1.   Position a rack in the center and preheat oven to 350°F. Line a

baking sheet with parchment paper (or use a nonstick baking sheet).

    2.   Using an electric mixer set at medium speed, cream the butter and sugar together in a large bowl until light and fluffy. Beat in the eggs, one at a time.

    3.   Blend in the vanilla, the unsweetened chocolate, and the sour cream. Fold in the chopped white chocolate.

    4.   In a large bowl, sift together the flour, cocoa, baking soda, baking powder, and salt. Mix into the butter mixture. Stir in the nuts. Drop rounded tablespoons of the dough onto the prepared sheet, spacing them 2 inches apart. Bake until nearly firm but still soft to the touch in the center, about 10 minutes. Using a spatula, transfer the cookies to wire racks to cool completely. Store in an airtight container at room temperature.

Do ahead: The cookies can be made up to 1 week in advance.

MAKES 6 DOZEN COOKIES.

*The creator: Jon Jividen, executive
chef for Ridgewells Caterer Inc. in
King of Prussia, Pennsylvania*

Black and White Sandwiches

Here's an upscale, white chocolate version of one of America's all-time favorites: the Oreo. For best results, fill these cookies just before serving.

Cookies
12 tablespoons unsalted butter, at room temperature
¾ cup sugar
2 large eggs, at room temperature
1½ teaspoons vanilla extract
1½ cups flour
½ cup unsweetened cocoa powder (preferably Dutch process)
¼ teaspoon baking powder
¼ teaspoon baking soda
⅛ teaspoon salt
½ cup chopped walnuts

Ganache
1 cup heavy (whipping) cream
6 ounces finely chopped white chocolate

Make the cookies:

1.   Position a rack in the center and preheat oven to 350°F. Lightly butter three baking sheets or three sheets of aluminum foil. Using an electric mixer set at medium speed, cream the butter and sugar in a large

bowl. Add the eggs one at a time, beating well after each addition. Add the vanilla, and continue beating until blended.

2. Sift together the flour, cocoa powder, baking powder, baking soda, and salt onto a sheet of waxed paper. Using an electric mixer set at low speed, gradually add the flour mixture and then the walnuts to the egg mixture, mixing just until blended. Wrap the dough in plastic wrap and refrigerate until firm enough to be rolled out, at least 2 hours.

3. Divide the dough in thirds. Place one-third on a well floured surface, keeping the remainder refrigerated. Roll out the dough to a thickness of $\frac{1}{8}$-inch. Brush off excess flour with a soft, dry pastry brush. Cut out 2-inch rounds of dough with a fluted or plain cookie cutter dipped in flour. Using a floured spatula, transfer the cookies to the baking sheets, spacing them about $\frac{1}{2}$-inch apart. (This dough is quite soft and must be handled carefully; return the dough to the refrigerator if it becomes difficult to work with.) Repeat with remaining dough, and reroll chilled scraps.

4. Bake the cookies until set and centers are dry to the touch, about 10 to 12 minutes. Do not overbake. Transfer the cookies to a wire rack and cool completely. The cookies will become crisp as they cool.

Make the ganache:

5. In a heavy medium saucepan over medium-high heat, bring the cream to a boil. Add the white chocolate and remove from heat. Let the mixture stand briefly; stir until smooth. Transfer to a metal bowl and refrigerate until chilled thoroughly, stirring occasionally. (To speed the process, place the metal bowl in a larger bowl of ice water; stir the chocolate mixture until cool.) With a whisk or an electric mixer, whip the white chocolate mixture just until fluffy, about 1 minute. Refrigerate until chilled, about 30 minutes. Whip until thickened, about 1 minute. Do not overwhip.

Assemble:

6. With a small spatula, spread about 2 teaspoons of ganache on

the flat sides of half of the cookies. Top each coated cookie with a plain cookie, pressing the flat bottoms lightly onto the ganache. Store up to 1 hour at cool room temperature before serving. (In warm weather, these cookies should be refrigerated. Refrigerate any remaining filled cookies.)

Do ahead: The cocoa cookies can be made up to 2 days in advance and stored at room temperature in an airtight container. The ganache can be made and refrigerated up to 1 day in advance.

MAKES ABOUT 32 SANDWICHES.

The creator: Richard Sax,
food writer, magazine columnist,
and cookbook author

Marble Swirl Truffles

⁓

These golf ball–sized truffles make a dramatic and elegant presentation. Note that the white chocolate layer will be softer in texture than the dark, adding another dimension to this sophisticated recipe.

Dark chocolate layer
3 tablespoons heavy (whipping) cream
1 tablespoon unsalted butter
4 ounces finely chopped semisweet chocolate
¼ teaspoon vanilla extract

White chocolate layer
3 tablespoons heavy (whipping) cream

1 tablespoon crème fraîche (see index)
5 ounces finely chopped white chocolate
Unsweetened cocoa powder (preferably Dutch process)

Dipping
19 ounces finely chopped semisweet chocolate
8 ounces finely chopped white chocolate

Make the dark chocolate layer:
1. In a heavy small saucepan over medium heat, bring the cream and butter to a simmer, stirring frequently. Reduce the heat to low. Add the semisweet chocolate and vanilla and whisk until smooth.
2. Pour mixture into small 8-inch round or square glass cake pan. Freeze until firm, about 20 minutes.

Make the white chocolate layer:
3. In a heavy small saucepan over medium heat, bring the cream to a simmer, stirring frequently. Reduce the heat to low. Stir in the crème

fraîche and mix until smooth; do not boil. Add the white chocolate and stir until smooth. Cool mixture slightly.

4. Pour the white chocolate mixture over the dark chocolate layer. Freeze until the mixture is firm enough to hold a shape, about 15 minutes.

5. Line a baking sheet with waxed paper and dust generously with cocoa powder. Spoon 12 mounds of the chocolate layers onto the prepared sheet, each mound consisting of 2 tablespoons of chocolate. (Make sure to get equal amounts of white and dark chocolate.) Freeze until the centers are almost firm, about 10 minutes.

6. Roll each mound in cocoa powder on the baking sheet, then roll between the palms of your hands into a smooth round. Set on another clean waxed paper-lined baking sheet and freeze at least 2 hours before dipping.

Dip the truffles:

7. In a double boiler over hot—not simmering—water, melt 1 pound of the semisweet chocolate until it registers 115°F on a candy thermometer. As the chocolate melts and the water cools, replace the cool water with hot water, as needed. Place the double boiler in front of you on the counter. Line a baking sheet with waxed paper. Completely submerge one truffle in the melted chocolate. Scoop out the truffle using a regular dinner fork, and tap it gently on the rim of the pan, allowing the excess chocolate to drip back into the pan. Gently drop the truffle onto the prepared sheet. Repeat process with remaining truffles. (Note: Take the temperature of the chocolate halfway through the dipping process to ensure that it is between 115°F and 120°F. If temperature drops below 115°F, reheat by replacing water with hot water and stirring.) Refrigerate until the chocolate is set, about 1 hour.

8. In a double boiler over hot—not simmering—water, melt the white chocolate until it registers 115°F on a candy thermometer. Place the double boiler in front of you on the counter. Grasp one side of a cold

truffle between your thumb and index finger. Dip the truffle halfway into the white chocolate. Immediately brush the bottom of the truffle along a piece of waxed paper to remove any excess white chocolate. Set on another waxed paper–lined baking sheet. Repeat the process with the remaining truffles. Refrigerate until set, about 1 hour.

9. In a double boiler over hot—not simmering—water, melt the remaining semisweet chocolate, stirring frequently. Using a fork, drizzle streaks of the semisweet chocolate over the truffles. Refrigerate until the chocolate is set, about 1 hour.

10. After the truffles are set, using rubber gloves or plastic wrap to prevent finger prints, place in appropriately sized paper or foil candy cups. Arrange cups in an airtight container and refrigerate. Remove from the refrigerator about 30 minutes before serving.

Do ahead: The truffles can be made and refrigerated up to 1 week in advance, and frozen up to 2 months.

MAKES 12 TRUFFLES.

The creator: Sarah Tenaglia,
assistant editor for
Bon Appétit *magazine*

Triple Chocolate Peanut Clusters

The creator of these clusters, unable to keep up with sales demand, finally revealed her secret recipe. What makes them so delicious is the blend of chocolates. There is more white chocolate than milk and semisweet, and that makes their texture so unbelievably creamy. This recipe can be halved and the chocolates can be melted in a double boiler instead of a frying pan.

2 pounds finely chopped white chocolate

1 12-ounce package semisweet chocolate chips

1 12-ounce package milk chocolate chips

1 24-ounce jar unsalted dry-roasted peanuts

1. In an electric frying pan on the lowest setting, melt the white chocolate with the chocolate chips, stirring constantly to blend. Cool 5 minutes. Stir in the peanuts.
2. Drop the mixture by tablespoonfuls onto waxed paper. Cool completely. Wrap airtight in plastic and refrigerate until ready to serve.

Do ahead: The clusters can be made and refrigerated up to 1 month ahead.

MAKES ABOUT 7 DOZEN CLUSTERS.

*The creator: Gayle McQuown, a home cook
who resides in Orange, California*

*At right: Mock Hostess Cupcakes
On following page: Black and White Soufflé*

7
Soufflés, Puddings, and Crepes

White Chocolate Soufflés

Serve these heavenly individual soufflés with softly whipped cream.

6 tablespoons milk
½ cup sugar
4 large egg yolks, at room
    temperature
6 large egg whites, at room
    temperature
½ teaspoon lemon juice
8 ounces finely chopped white
    chocolate, melted and tepid
Confectioners' sugar, for garnish

1.   Position a rack in the center and preheat oven to 350°F. Butter four 4½-inch diameter (2 cup) soufflé dishes and sprinkle sugar on the bottoms and sides. Discard excess sugar.

2.   In a heavy small saucepan over medium heat, combine the milk and sugar, stirring constantly to dissolve the sugar. Remove from heat and whisk in the egg yolks.

3.   Using an electric mixer set at low speed, beat the egg whites with the lemon juice in a grease-free medium bowl until they start to foam. Gradually increase the speed to high and continue beating the egg whites until they form stiff peaks.

4.   Using an electric mixer, beat the white chocolate into the milk mixture until smooth. Fold one-fourth of the beaten egg whites into the

milk mixture to lighten it; carefully fold in the remaining beaten egg whites.

5.   Gently spoon an equal amount of the mixture into each of the prepared soufflé dishes. Bake until the soufflés are puffed and the tops are firm and shake only slightly when the oven rack is gently moved, about 18 to 20 minutes. Do not open the oven door until the soufflés are done. Sprinkle with confectioners' sugar and serve immediately.

MAKES 4 SERVINGS.

White Chocolate Pots de Crème

Looks can be deceiving: these pots de crème appear to be vanilla in flavor, but they taste like white chocolate.

Pots de crème
¼ cup sugar
1 large egg, at room temperature
1 large egg yolk, at room
  temperature
1 cup milk, tepid
2½ ounces finely chopped white
  chocolate, melted and tepid

Garnish
Whipped cream
Candied violets
White chocolate shavings (see index)

1. Position a rack in the center and preheat oven to 300°F. In a bowl, using a wire whisk, combine the sugar, egg, and egg yolk. Gradually whisk the milk into the egg mixture. Whisk in the melted white chocolate. Strain the mixture through a fine-mesh sieve into a bowl.

2. Set four 6-ounce custard cups in a large shallow baking dish. Pour the mixture into the cups, dividing it evenly among them. Place the pan with the cups into the preheated oven. Add enough nearly boiling water to the pan to come halfway up the sides of the cups. Bake until the

tops are nearly set and move slightly when pan is moved gently, or until a cake tester gently inserted about ½ inch from the edge of the cups comes out clean, about 45 minutes.

3. Remove cups from the water and let cool to room temperature on a rack. Refrigerate, covered, for at least 4 hours or overnight. Garnish each cup with a dollop or rosette of whipped cream, a candied violet, or white chocolate shavings, if desired.

Do ahead: Make the pots de crème up to 1 day in advance.

MAKES 4 SERVINGS.

*The creator: Roland Liccioni,
chef for Carlos' Restaurant in
Highland Park, Illinois*

White Chocolate Tortoni

This decidedly rich dessert is heady with marsala, yet the white chocolate flavor is distinctive.

8 ounces cream cheese, at room
    temperature
½ cup confectioners' sugar
⅓ cup sweet marsala wine
1 teaspoon vanilla extract
4 ounces grated white chocolate
1 cup heavy (whipping) cream,
    chilled
2 large egg whites, at room
    temperature
1 cup crushed amaretti cookies
    (about 20 cookies)

1.   In a food processor fitted with a metal blade, blend the cream cheese, confectioners' sugar, wine, and vanilla until smooth. Transfer to a large bowl and fold in the white chocolate.

2.   In a chilled small bowl, whip the cream until nearly stiff. Using an electric mixer fitted with clean, dry beaters and set at low speed, beat the egg whites in a grease-free small bowl until they start to foam. Gradually increase the speed to high and continue beating until the egg whites form stiff peaks. Stir one-third of the whipped cream into the cream cheese mixture to lighten it, then fold in the remaining whipped cream.

Stir one-third of the beaten egg whites into the cream cheese mixture to lighten it, then fold in the remaining egg whites.

3.   Divide half of the mixture among eight 1-cup ramekins or pot de crème pots. Top each with 1 tablespoon of crushed cookies. Divide the remaining mixture among the ramekins, covering the cookies completely. Top each with an equal amount of the remaining crushed cookies. Cover and refrigerate overnight or at least 4 hours.

Do ahead: The tortoni can be made and refrigerated up to 2 days in advance.

MAKES 8 SERVINGS.

The creator: Joyce Resnik,
recipe tester for
Bon Appétit *magazine*
and food writer

White Chocolate Bread Pudding with Brandied Apricots and Pecans

In this recipe, the impact of white chocolate is quite subtle. Just when you begin to wonder why you can't taste it, suddenly you'll recognize it. This homey pudding is a little denser than most, and there's plenty of crunch from the pecans and apricots to add textural intrigue.

5 ounces finely chopped white
   chocolate
2 cups half-and-half
½ loaf (5 ounces) day-old French
   bread, cut into ½-inch cubes
   (about 3½ cups)
⅓ cup plus 1 teaspoon brandy
½ cup coarsely chopped dried
   apricots
3 large eggs
½ cup coarsely chopped pecans
Whipped cream flavored with
   brandy, for garnish (optional)

1.   Butter an 8″ × 10½″ × 1½″ baking pan. In a double boiler over hot—not simmering—water, melt the white chocolate, stirring frequently. In a large saucepan, heat the half-and-half to a boil. Whisk the half-and-

half into the white chocolate. Place the French bread cubes in a large bowl. Stir in the white chocolate mixture and let stand for 45 minutes.

2.   In a small saucepan over medium heat, bring ⅓ cup of the brandy with the apricots to a simmer. Remove from heat and let cool for 15 minutes. Drain the apricots, reserving the liquid for later use.

3.   Position a rack in the center and preheat oven to 325°F. In a medium bowl, whisk the eggs until they are smooth. Whisk in the drained soaking brandy plus the remaining teaspoon and stir in the pecans. Stir the egg mixture into the white chocolate–bread mixture. Stir in the apricots.

4.   Pour the mixture into the prepared pan. Set inside a larger pan. Pour enough boiling water into the larger pan to come halfway up the sides of the prepared pan. Bake until the tip of a knife inserted one-third from the pan edge comes out clean, about 50 to 55 minutes. Serve at room temperature with freshly whipped cream flavored with brandy, if desired.

Do ahead: The bread pudding can be made up to 1 day in advance and refrigerated. Bring to room temperature before serving.

MAKES 8 SERVINGS.

*The creator: Patrick O'Connell,
chef/co-owner of The Inn at Little
Washington in Washington, Virginia*

White Chocolate Steamed Pudding

◈

White chocolate works beautifully in a classic steamed pudding: it accentuates the smooth, moist texture. It's delicious served with fresh strawberries and mint leaves as garnish. Traditionally, however, it's served with a sauce, so you can present each slice in a pool of white chocolate crème Anglaise (see index). Or, top individual servings with a dollop of softly whipped cream lightly flavored with amaretto or brandy.

¼ pound unsalted butter, at room temperature
4 ounces coarsely chopped white chocolate, melted and tepid
4 large eggs, separated, at room temperature
½ cup sugar, divided
½ cup flour, sifted
¾ cup finely ground almonds
6 ladyfingers, homemade or store-bought, crumbled (about 1 cup)

1.   Butter a 5-cup pudding mold and dust it with sugar. Using an electric mixer set at medium speed, beat the butter in a large bowl until fluffy. Beat in the melted white chocolate. Beat in the egg yolks and ¼ cup of the sugar until smooth.

2. Using an electric mixer fitted with clean beaters and set at low speed, beat the egg whites in a grease-free medium bowl until they start to foam. Gradually increase the speed to high and continue beating the egg whites until they form soft peaks. Gradually beat in the remaining ¼ cup sugar and continue beating until the egg whites form stiff peaks. Fold one-fourth of the beaten egg whites into the white chocolate mixture to lighten it; fold in the remaining egg whites.

3. Fold in the flour, almonds, and ladyfingers. Spoon the mixture into the prepared pan. Fold a clean dish towel and place on the bottom of a large saucepan. Set the mold in the saucepan. Fill the saucepan with enough water to come halfway up the sides of the mold. Cover the saucepan with a tight-fitting lid. Over high heat, bring the water to a boil, then reduce the heat to low and let the pudding steam until a cake tester inserted in the center of the pudding comes out clean, about 1 hour and 45 minutes.

4. Remove the mold and let cool slightly on a wire rack. Run a knife around the edges of the mold and invert the pudding onto a serving platter. Serve warm.

Do ahead: The pudding can be made up to 2 days in advance and refrigerated. Bring to room temperature before reheating. To reheat, wrap tightly in aluminum foil and steam until heated through, about 20 minutes.

MAKES 6 SERVINGS.

White Chocolate Crème Caramel

What makes a smooth crème caramel smoother? White chocolate, of course.

Caramel
1 cup sugar
½ cup water

Custard
1 quart milk
*5 ounces finely chopped white
    chocolate*
6 large eggs, at room temperature
1 cup sugar

Make the caramel:

1. Position a rack in the center and preheat oven to 325°F. In a heavy medium saucepan over low heat, combine the sugar and water; stir until the sugar dissolves. Increase the heat to medium-high and boil the syrup, brushing down the sugar crystals from the sides of the pan with water, until the mixture turns a rich golden brown. Pour an equal amount of caramel into the bottom of eight 8-ounce ramekins and set aside to harden.

Make the custard:

2. In a heavy large saucepan over high heat, bring the milk to a boil. Remove the milk from the heat and whisk in the white chocolate, stirring until it's melted. Using an electric mixer set at medium speed, beat

the eggs and sugar in a large bowl until light and fluffy. Using an electric mixer set at medium speed, gradually beat the milk mixture into the egg mixture. Use a spoon to skim off any froth.

3.   Set the ramekins in a large, shallow baking pan. Pour an equal amount of the custard into each ramekin. Add enough boiling water to the baking pan to come halfway up the sides of the ramekins. Bake until a knife inserted on the edge of a ramekin comes clean, about 35 to 45 minutes. Transfer the custard cups to a wire rack to cool. Refrigerate, covered, overnight.

4.   To unmold the crème caramels, use a sharp knife to loosen the custard from the sides of the ramekins and invert each onto the center of a serving plate.

Do ahead: The crème caramels can be made up to 1 day in advance.

MAKES 8 SERVINGS.

The creator: Marjorie L. Kuerer,
chef of the Black Pearl Restaurant in
Providence, Rhode Island

White Chocolate–Almond Crepes with Chartreuse Crème Anglaise

❧

White chocolate acts as a sweetener and texture enhancer in this elegant recipe. This is a fine dessert to serve at dinner parties; every component can be made in advance and assembled just before serving. If you like, you may substitute fresh raspberries or other fruit for the papaya.

Crepes
1 cup flour
3 tablespoons sugar
1¼ cups milk
3 large eggs, beaten
2 tablespoons unsalted butter, melted
Pinch of salt
Dash of vanilla extract
Pinch of cinnamon
¼ cup finely chopped toasted almonds (see index)
Melted butter, for cooking crepes

Crème Anglaise
6 large egg yolks
½ cup sugar
1½ cups heavy (whipping) cream
1 ounce Chartreuse, or to taste

Filling
1 envelope unflavored gelatin
¼ cup water
4½ ounces finely chopped white chocolate
5 large egg yolks, at room temperature
⅔ cup sugar
1 teaspoon kirsch
7 large egg whites, at room temperature
¼ cup finely chopped toasted almonds (see index)
1 large, very ripe, sweet papaya, peeled, seeded, and diced

Garnish
Confectioners' sugar
1 medium, very ripe, sweet papaya, peeled, seeded, and thinly sliced
10 fresh mint leaves

Make the crepes:

1. Sift the flour and sugar into a large bowl. Slowly mix in 1 cup of the milk, eggs, butter, salt, vanilla, and cinnamon until smooth. Let the batter rest 1 hour; stir in the remaining milk and almonds.

2. Place a 6-inch skillet over medium heat until hot. Using a pastry brush, lightly brush the pan with some melted butter. Pour 2 tablespoons of crepe batter into skillet; swirl the pan to distribute the batter thinly and evenly, covering the bottom of the skillet.

3. Cook the crepe about 1 to 2 minutes on each side, until the edges are firm and light brown. Invert the crepe onto a plate and cover with a sheet of waxed paper. Lightly brush the skillet with additional butter and repeat the procedure until all the batter is used.

Make the crème Anglaise:

4. In a bowl, beat the egg yolks and sugar together until combined. In a saucepan over medium heat, bring the cream to a slow boil. Whisk ½ cup hot cream into the egg yolk and sugar mixture. Pour the mixture back into the saucepan and continue cooking on low heat until it thickens enough to coat the back of a spoon. Remove from the heat and stir in the Chartreuse. Let cool and refrigerate, covered, at least 2 hours.

Make the filling:

5. In a large bowl, soften gelatin in ¼ cup water. In a double boiler over hot—not simmering—water, melt the white chocolate, stirring frequently until smooth. Remove from heat. Stir the white chocolate into the gelatin until dissolved.

6. Using an electric mixer set at medium speed, beat the egg yolks and ⅓ cup sugar in a grease-free large bowl until they become pale yellow and form a thick ribbon when the beaters are lifted. Fold into the white chocolate mixture. Stir in the kirsch.

7. In a heavy small saucepan over low heat, combine the remaining ⅓ cup sugar with just enough water to dilute the sugar; stir until the sugar dissolves. Increase the heat to medium-high and boil the syrup, brushing down sugar crystals from the sides of the pan with water, until the mixture

registers 238°F on a candy thermometer, about 5 to 10 minutes.

8. Meanwhile, using a heavy-duty mixer set at low speed, beat the egg whites until foamy. Gradually increase the speed to high and continue beating until they start to form soft peaks. Gradually beat in the sugar syrup and continue beating until cool and stiff. Fold into the white chocolate mixture. Fold in the chopped almonds.

Assemble:

9. Spoon 2 tablespoons of the filling on one side of each crepe. Sprinkle each crepe with about 2 teaspoons papaya. Gently roll the crepe around filling. Place the crepes in a large baking pan in a 350°F oven until warmed through, about 10 minutes. Place crepes on dessert plates, allowing two per serving.

10. Spoon about 3 tablespoons of crème Anglaise over each serving. Sift confectioners' sugar over each crepe. Garnish each plate with papaya slices and a fresh mint leaf. Serve immediately.

Do ahead: The crepes may be wrapped in aluminum foil and refrigerated up to 3 days or frozen up to 3 months. The crème Anglaise and the white chocolate filling can be made and refrigerated up to 1 day in advance.

MAKES 10 SERVINGS.

The creator: Daniel Thiebaut,
executive chef for The Mauna Kea
Beach Hotel in Kamuela, Hawaii

At right: White Chocolate Madeleines
On following page: Winter White Pie

8
Cookies,
Brownies,
Quick Breads,
and
Confections

White Chocolate Cocomacs

2 cups flour
1 teaspoon baking soda
1 teaspoon salt
½ pound unsalted butter, at room
temperature
1 cup packed dark brown sugar
¼ cup packed light brown sugar
¼ cup sugar
2 large eggs, at room temperature
2½ teaspoons vanilla extract
¾ cup unsalted, coarsely chopped
macadamia nuts
12 ounces coarsely chopped white
chocolate
1⅓ cups sweetened shredded coconut

1. In a medium bowl, sift together the flour, baking soda, and salt. Using an electric mixer set at medium speed, cream the butter, brown sugars, and sugar in a large bowl. Add the eggs and vanilla and beat until the mixture is light and fluffy. Beat in the flour mixture until just combined; do not overbeat. Stir in the macadamia nuts, white chocolate, and coconut. Cover the dough with plastic wrap and refrigerate at least 2 hours.

2. Position a rack in the center and preheat oven to 350°F. Line a baking sheet with parchment paper. Using a 2⅜-inch diameter ice cream scoop to form the cookies, pack the dough into the scoop so it is even with the edge. Release the dough onto the center of the baking sheet. Place four

scoops evenly spaced around the center scoop. Bake in the preheated oven until the cookies are golden around the edges (the centers will be soft), about 18 to 20 minutes. Transfer the cookies in the pan to a rack and cool until they are just warm. The cookies will become slightly crisp around the edges as they cool. Transfer the cookies to a wire rack and cool completely. Repeat with the remaining dough, using cool baking sheets. Store cookies in an airtight container at room temperature.

Do ahead: The dough can be prepared and refrigerated up to 2 days before baking. The cookies can be made up to 2 days in advance.

MAKES ABOUT 20 COOKIES.

The creator: Marcia M. Tunison,
who won second prize with this recipe
in Chocolatier *magazine's annual*
Great Chocolate Challenge contest

White Chocolate Madeleines

Reportedly, the original madeleines were created by the pastry chef for Talleyrand, the famed French statesman. This variation proves how a good dessert gets better. The white chocolate flavor is subtly apparent, yet the classic madeleine texture is maintained. You can drizzle the madeleines with white chocolate only, but the dark chocolate contributes color contrast.

Madeleines

4 ounces finely chopped white
    chocolate
12 tablespoons unsalted butter
4 large eggs
⅔ cup sugar
¼ teaspoon salt
1 cup flour

Glaze

2 ounces finely chopped white
    chocolate
1 tablespoon confectioners' sugar
1½ tablespoons vegetable oil
2 ounces finely chopped semisweet
    chocolate, melted (optional)

Make the madeleines:
1. Position a rack in the center and preheat oven to 350°F. Butter

two number 80 madeleine pans. (You can use any size, but fill the individual madeleines two-thirds full.) If you have only one pan, bake one batch at a time, allowing the pan to cool after each baking.

2. In a double boiler over hot—not simmering—water, melt the white chocolate with the butter, stirring frequently.

3. In a medium metal bowl, combine the eggs with the sugar. Set the bowl over a pan of barely simmering water, whisking constantly until the mixture is warm to the touch and the sugar has dissolved, about 1 minute. Remove the bowl from water. Using an electric mixer set at high speed, beat the egg mixture with the salt until it is pale yellow and forms a thick ribbon when the beaters are lifted. Reduce the speed to low. Sprinkle the flour over the egg mixture and beat until just blended, about 3 to 4 seconds. Add the white chocolate mixture and continue beating until almost incorporated. Using a rubber spatula, finish folding the batter by hand until smooth.

4. Spoon the batter into the prepared molds and bake until the madeleines are firm when lightly touched in the center, about 12 to 15 minutes. Immediately invert madeleines onto a wire rack and cool completely. (Note: If madeleines begin to stick before all are removed, return the pan to the oven just long enough to reheat the pan, and then remove the remaining madeleines.)

Make the glaze:

5. In a double boiler over hot—not simmering—water, melt the white chocolate with the confectioners' sugar, stirring frequently. Remove the pan from water. Stir in the vegetable oil.

Assemble:

6. Using a fork, drizzle streaks of white chocolate glaze over the madeleines. If desired, drizzle the melted semisweet chocolate over madeleines, decoratively overlapping the white chocolate design.

Do ahead: The glazed madeleines can be made up to 8 hours in advance and kept at cool room temperature. Unglazed madeleines can be made and kept in an airtight container for 2 days, or frozen up to 1 month.

MAKES 4 DOZEN MADELEINES.

The creator: Marion Cunningham,
author of numerous cookbooks
and culinary consultant

White Chocolate Chip Crisps

These are thin, crispy cookies made to be dunked into hot chocolate or milk. Not only will children enjoy them, but the recipe is so easy, they can make them themselves.

½ pound unsalted butter, melted
1 cup packed light brown sugar
1 cup sugar
2 large eggs, at room temperature
1 teaspoon vanilla extract
2 cups flour
1¼ teaspoons baking powder
1 teaspoon baking soda

1 cup quick-cooking oats
1 cup cornflakes, crushed
1 cup (6 ounces) white chocolate chips
1 cup chopped, toasted walnuts (see index)
½ cup sweetened shredded coconut

1. Position a rack in the center and preheat oven to 350°F. Using an electric mixer at medium speed, blend the butter and sugars in a large bowl until light and fluffy. Beat in the eggs, one at a time, then add the vanilla and blend thoroughly.

2. In a large bowl, combine the flour with the baking powder and soda. Mix in the oats and cornflakes. Mix into the butter mixture. Fold in the white chocolate chips, walnuts, and coconut. Drop by rounded tablespoonfuls onto ungreased baking sheets about two inches apart. Bake until cookies spread to a flat, round shape and are lightly browned, about 12 minutes. Transfer the cookies to wire racks and cool completely. Store in an airtight container at room temperature.

Do ahead: The cookies can be made up to 1 week in advance.

MAKES ABOUT 8 DOZEN COOKIES.

White Chocolate–Pecan Crescents

These rich little pastries are quite like rugelach, the crescent-shaped cookies that are so popular in European and American Jewish communities. They're wonderful served at brunch, for a coffee break, well, what the heck—they're great to snack on anytime.

Cookies
½ pound unsalted butter, at room
   temperature
½ pound cream cheese, at room
   temperature
2 cups flour
2 tablespoons sugar

Filling
½ cup sugar
1 tablespoon cinnamon
1 cup finely chopped toasted pecans
   (see index)
1 cup dried currants
1 cup (6 ounces) white chocolate
   chips

Coating
1 pound finely chopped white
   chocolate, melted and tepid

Make the cookies:

1.   Using an electric mixer set at medium speed, beat the butter, cream cheese, flour, and sugar in a large bowl until well blended and dough pulls away from the sides of the bowl. Divide the dough into four pieces and flatten each piece between two pieces of waxed paper. Refrigerate until well chilled, about 1 hour.

Make the filling:

2.   Position a rack in the center and preheat oven to 350°F. Line two baking sheets with parchment paper. In a large bowl, combine the sugar, cinnamon, pecans, currants, and white chocolate chips.

Assemble:

3.   Remove the dough from the refrigerator. Roll out one piece of dough to form a 12-inch circle. Using a pastry brush, spread one-fourth of the melted white chocolate evenly over the circle. Quickly and evenly sprinkle one-fourth of the filling on the circle. Using a very sharp knife or a pizza cutter, cut the circle into 12 triangles. Roll each triangle from the outer edge to the center, to form crescent shapes. Place them 2 inches apart on the prepared baking sheets. Repeat the process with the three remaining pieces of dough. Bake until golden brown and puffed, about 23 to 25 minutes. Transfer the pastries in the pan to wire racks and cool completely. Store in an airtight container.

Do ahead: The pastries can be made up to 1 week in advance and frozen up to 1 month.

MAKES 4 DOZEN COOKIES.

Two-for-One
Peanut Butter Cookies

~~~~~

This recipe is really two for one; it should please those who love chewy cookies and those who love chunky ones. White chocolate is melted into half of the dough to create a chewy cookie with a cracked, shiny surface and a subtle white chocolate flavor. The remaining white chocolate is folded in pieces into the dough for a chunkier variation with a pronounced white chocolate taste. No matter which you prefer, you'll agree that the salty taste of peanut butter is a fine foil for the sweetness of white chocolate.

½ cup smooth peanut butter
¼ cup unsalted butter, at room
   temperature
½ cup sugar
¼ cup packed brown sugar
1 large egg, at room temperature
¾ cup flour
1 teaspoon baking soda
5 ounces coarsely chopped white
   chocolate, divided

1.   Position a rack in the center and preheat oven to 400°F. Lightly butter two baking sheets. Using an electric mixer set at medium speed, cream the butters and sugars in a large bowl until smooth. Beat in the egg until incorporated.

2. In a small bowl, combine the flour and the baking soda. Beat the flour mixture into the butter mixture. Cover and refrigerate the dough for 10 minutes.

3. In a double boiler over hot—not simmering—water, melt half of the white chocolate, stirring frequently. Cool to room temperature.

4. Remove the dough from the refrigerator and divide it into two equal parts. Place half of the dough into a medium bowl. Using an electric mixer set at medium speed, blend the melted white chocolate into the dough.

5. Place the remaining dough in a medium bowl. Using an electric mixer set at medium speed, blend the chopped white chocolate into the dough.

7. Roll the dough into 1-inch balls. Place the dough balls on the prepared baking sheets about 1 inch apart. The cookies will puff and spread slightly. Bake until light golden in color, about 6 to 8 minutes. Transfer the cookies to a wire rack and cool completely. Store in an airtight container.

Do ahead: The peanut butter cookies can be made up to 2 days in advance.

MAKES ABOUT 34 COOKIES.

The creator: Joan Steuer, president of Chocolate Marketing, Inc., a New York–based marketing and consulting firm for chocolate and dessert companies

White Chocolate–Hazelnut Cookies

〰️

It's easy to be enthusiastic about these big, rich, and buttery cookies: they offer a double whammy of white chocolate. Some of it is melted into the batter, while the remaining is folded in in chunks. The cookies resemble the typical, popular chocolate chip variety, but once you try them, you can immediately taste the delicious difference.

⅟₄ pound unsalted butter
12 ounces coarsely chopped white
    chocolate
2 large eggs, at room temperature
⅓ cup packed brown sugar
⅓ cup sugar
1½ teaspoons vanilla extract
4 ounces cream cheese
1¾ cups flour
1¼ teaspoons baking soda
¼ teaspoon cinnamon
8 ounces coarsely chopped semisweet
    chocolate
½ cup coarsely chopped hazelnuts

1. Position a rack in the center and preheat oven to 350°F. Lightly butter baking sheets. In a double boiler over hot—not simmering—water,

melt the butter and 8 ounces of the white chocolate, stirring frequently. Set aside and let cool until tepid.

2.   In a large bowl, beat the eggs until light and frothy. Beat in the sugars until the mixture is light and fluffy, about 3 minutes. Blend in the tepid white chocolate mixture and the vanilla.

3.   In a double boiler over simmering water, melt the cream cheese, stirring occasionally. Blend into the white chocolate mixture. In a medium bowl, combine the flour, baking soda, and cinnamon; blend into the white chocolate mixture. Fold in the remaining white chocolate, semisweet chocolate, and hazelnuts. Spoon by heaping tablespoonfuls, two inches apart, onto the prepared pans and bake until golden brown and firm to the touch, about 8 to 10 minutes. Transfer the cookies to wire racks and cool completely. Store in an airtight container at room temperature.

Do ahead: The cookies can be made up to 2 days in advance.

MAKES ABOUT 40 COOKIES.

The creator: Ann M. Bartholamay,
executive chef for Omni Nassau Inn
in Princeton, New Jersey

White Chocolate Brownies with White and Dark Chocolate Chunks

This recipe demonstrates how well white chocolate can enhance the texture of a dessert. Even though the brownies are wonderfully moist and possess a cake-like crumb, they're also chewy. It's best not to eat them straight from the oven; they're better served at room temperature or chilled. They freeze well, too. Actually, in case you're suddenly seized with a white chocolate craving, it's helpful to know that they taste equally great in their frozen state.

½ *pound unsalted butter, at room
    temperature*
1 *pound coarsely chopped white
    chocolate*
4 *large eggs, at room temperature*
1 *cup sugar*
1 *tablespoon vanilla extract*
Pinch of salt
2 *cups flour*
⅔ *cup chopped walnuts*
8 *ounces coarsely chopped
    bittersweet or semisweet chocolate*

1.   Position a rack in the center and preheat oven to 350°F. Line a 15″ × 11″ jelly roll pan with aluminum foil. Butter the foil.

2.   In a heavy medium saucepan over low heat, melt the butter.

Remove from heat and add half of the white chocolate. Do not stir. Cover and set aside.

3.   Using an electric mixer set at medium speed, beat the eggs and sugar in a large bowl until light and fluffy. Stir in the vanilla and the salt. Using a rubber spatula, carefully fold in the unstirred butter–white chocolate mixture. Carefully fold in the flour, then the walnuts. Fold in the remaining white and dark chocolate. Spread the batter evenly in the prepared pan.

4.   Bake until the center of the brownies springs back when lightly touched, and they are golden brown, about 35 minutes; do not overbake. (Brownies should be moist.) Transfer the brownies in the pan to a wire rack and cool completely. Using a sharp knife, cut the brownies into 32 squares.

MAKES 32 BROWNIES.

*The creator: Mark Militello,
executive chef for Cafe Max in
Pompano Beach, Maxaluna in
Boca Raton, and Max's Place in
North Miami, Florida*

Cashew-Praline Blondies

✦

Here's a sophisticated version of homey "blondies."

Praline

¼ cup sugar

2 tablespoons brandy or rum

4 ounces (about ¾ cup) unsalted
 roasted cashews (see index)

Blondies

3 ounces finely chopped white
 chocolate

4 tablespoons unsalted butter, at
 room temperature

½ cup packed light brown sugar

1 large egg, at room temperature

¾ teaspoon salt

1 tablespoon brandy or rum

1 cup flour

Topping

1½ ounces grated white chocolate

Make the praline:

1.   Lightly butter a baking sheet. In a heavy saucepan over low heat, combine the sugar and liquor. Stir until the sugar dissolves. Increase the heat to medium-high and boil the syrup, brushing the sugar crystals from the sides of the pan with water, until the syrup caramelizes. Immedi-

ately add the cashews and stir to coat with syrup. Quickly pour the mixture onto the prepared sheet, and cool competely. In a food processor fitted with a metal blade, finely chop the praline in batches, using on–off pulses.

Make the blondies:

2.   Position a rack in the center and preheat oven to 350°F. Butter an 8-inch square baking pan. Lightly dust the pan with flour; tap out the excess.

3.   In a double boiler set over hot—not simmering—water, melt the white chocolate, stirring frequently. Remove the pan from the water and cool to room temperature. Whisk in the butter 1 tablespoon at a time.

4.   Using an electric mixer set at high speed, beat the brown sugar, egg, and salt in a large bowl until it forms a thick ribbon when the beaters are lifted. Reduce the speed to low and beat in the brandy or rum. Using a rubber spatula, fold in the white chocolate mixture. Stir in the flour and ⅓ cup of the praline. Spread the batter evenly into the prepared pan.

5.   Bake for 18 minutes. Sprinkle the blondies evenly with the remaining praline and bake until a cake tester inserted in the center comes out clean, about 6 minutes. Transfer the blondies in the pan to a wire rack. Sprinkle the hot blondies with the grated white chocolate. Cool completely. Using a sharp knife, cut the blondies into 2-inch squares. Store in an airtight container.

Do ahead: The blondies can be made up to 2 days in advance.

MAKES 16 SQUARES.

The creator: Leslie Weiner,
food editor for Forecast *magazine*
and cookbook author

161

Apricot, White Chocolate, and Walnut Scones

Not only are dried apricots and walnuts a stellar combination with white chocolate, but these scones are so packed with ingredients that you get a balance of flavors in each bite. Be careful not to overbake them, as they barely brown. To prepare a heart-shaped variation for Valentine's Day or other romantic celebrations, follow the instructions at the end of the recipe.

2 cups flour
⅓ cup sugar
2 teaspoons baking powder
½ teaspoon salt
4 tablespoons unsalted butter, well chilled and cut into ½-inch cubes
½ cup heavy (whipping) cream

1 large egg, lightly beaten
1½ teaspoons vanilla extract
6 ounces white chocolate, cut into ½-inch chunks
1 cup coarsely broken toasted walnuts (see index)
1 cup chopped dried apricots

1.   Position a rack in the center and preheat oven to 375°F. Line a baking sheet with parchment paper. Trace a 9-inch circle on the parchment.
2.   In a large bowl, stir together the flour, sugar, baking powder, and salt. Using a pastry blender or two knives, cut the butter into the dry ingredients until the mixture resembles coarse meal.
3.   In another large bowl, whisk together the cream, egg, and vanilla. Stir the liquid ingredients into the dry ingredients until combined.

162

Stir in the white chocolate, walnuts, and apricots. Use your fingers, if necessary, to combine.

4.   Pat the dough into the 9-inch circle on the prepared baking sheet. Cut into eight wedges. Bake until the tops are lightly browned, about 15 to 20 minutes. Transfer the scones on the baking sheet to a wire rack and cool for 5 minutes. Using a spatula, remove the scones to the wire rack and cool completely or serve warm. Store, loosely wrapped, at room temperature.

To make scone hearts:

On a lightly floured work surface, pat the dough to a thickness of about ⅝ inch. Using a 3¼-inch heart-shaped cookie cutter, cut the dough into hearts. Gather the scraps of dough together and repeat until all the dough has been used to make hearts. Transfer the hearts to a parchment-lined baking sheet and bake as above.

Do ahead: The scones can be made up to 2 days in advance. Reheat, if desired.

MAKES 8 SCONES.

The creators: Barbara Albright,
editor-in-chief for Chocolatier
magazine and cookbook author;
Leslie Weiner, food editor for
Forecast *magazine and*
cookbook author

Macadamia Nut–White Chocolate Chip Muffins

These are not the trendy oversized muffins, but the homier, original ones. Taste them and discover that macadamia nuts and coconut possess a natural affinity with white chocolate.

2 cups flour
½ cup packed dark brown sugar
2 teaspoons baking powder
½ teaspoon salt
1 cup milk, at room temperature
8 tablespoons unsalted butter, melted and cooled
1 egg, at room temperature, lightly beaten
2 teaspoons vanilla extract
1¾ cups white chocolate chips
3½ ounces (scant ¾ cup) lightly salted, chopped macadamia nuts
¾ cup shredded toasted coconut

1.   Position a rack in the center and preheat oven to 400°F. Lightly butter twelve 3½- to 4-ounce muffin cups.
2.   In a large bowl, combine the flour, brown sugar, baking powder, and salt. In another bowl, whisk together the milk, butter, egg,

and vanilla. Make a well in the center of the dry ingredients. Gradually stir in the liquid ingredients just until combined. Stir in the white chocolate chips, macadamia nuts, and coconut.

3.   Spoon the batter into the prepared muffin cups, filling to the top. Bake until the muffins are a very light brown and a cake tester inserted into the center of one muffin comes out clean, about 20 minutes.

4.   Transfer the muffin tin or tins to a wire rack and cool for 5 minutes. Remove the muffins from the cups and cool completely on the rack. Serve warm or at room temperature. Store the muffins in an airtight container.

Do ahead: The muffins can be made up to 2 days in advance, and frozen up to 1 month.

MAKES 12 MUFFINS.

The creators: Barbara Albright,
editor-in-chief for Chocolatier
magazine and cookbook author;
Leslie Weiner, food editor for
Forecast *magazine and*
cookbook author

White Chocolate Shortbread

❦

The saying "the rich get richer" may even apply to desserts. Heaven knows, shortbread is quite rich, and with the bonus of white chocolate, it becomes even more so—what a delicious, decadent way to go.

4½ ounces coarsely chopped white
    chocolate
¼ pound unsalted butter, at room
    temperature
¼ cup firmly packed dark brown
    sugar
1 cup plus 2 tablespoons flour, sifted

1. Position a rack in the center and preheat oven to 400°F. Lightly butter a 9-inch pie pan. Using a food processor fitted with a metal blade, chop the white chocolate using on–off pulses, until it resembles coarse meal.

2. Using an electric mixer set at medium speed, cream the butter with the sugar in a large bowl until smooth. Beat in the flour. Stir in the chopped white chocolate.

3. Pat the dough evenly into the prepared pan. Using the tip of a sharp knife, score the dough into eight equal triangles.

4. Bake the shortbread until light golden in color, about 30 minutes. Transfer in the pan to a wire rack to cool slightly. Remove the shortbread from the pan and cool completely on the wire rack. Store in an airtight container at room temperature.

Do ahead: The shortbread can be made up to 2 weeks in advance, or frozen up to 1 month.

MAKES 8 SERVINGS.

*The creator: Joan Steuer, president
of Chocolate Marketing, Inc.,
a New York–based marketing
consulting firm for chocolate and
dessert companies*

White Chocolate Cupcakes

Fine-crumb white chocolate cupcakes are topped with thick swirls of white chocolate buttercream.

Cupcakes
3 ounces finely chopped white
   chocolate
¼ cup milk
½ cup heavy (whipping) cream
½ teaspoon vinegar
¼ pound unsalted butter, at room
   temperature
1 cup sugar
2 large eggs, separated, at room
   temperature
1¼ cups flour
1 teaspoon baking soda
¼ teaspoon salt

Icing
8 ounces finely chopped white
   chocolate
1 cup sugar
2 tablespoons cornstarch
½ cup boiling water
¾ pound unsalted butter, at room
   temperature

Make the cupcakes:

1. Position a rack in the middle and preheat oven to 350°F. Line 16 muffin cups with paper baking cups.

2. In a double boiler over hot—not simmering—water, melt the white chocolate, stirring frequently. In a heavy small saucepan over medium-high heat, bring the milk to a boil and beat it into the white chocolate. In a small bowl, combine the cream and vinegar; set aside.

3. Using an electric mixer set at medium speed, cream the butter

and sugar in a large bowl until light and fluffy. Beat in the egg yolks one at a time, beating well after each addition. Stir the white chocolate mixture into the butter mixture.

4. Into a medium bowl, sift the flour, baking soda, and salt. Beat the flour mixture into the white chocolate mixture, alternating with the cream mixture, until smooth.

5. In a grease-free medium bowl, using an electric mixer set at low speed, beat the egg whites until they start to foam. Gradually increase the speed to high. Continue beating until the egg whites form stiff peaks. Fold one-fourth of the beaten egg whites into the white chocolate mixture to lighten it; fold in the remaining egg whites.

6. Spoon an equal amount of batter into each of the 16 cups and bake until a cake tester inserted in the center of a cupcake comes out clean and the cupcake tops are golden, about 25 to 30 minutes. Transfer the cupcakes in the pan(s) to a wire rack to cool for 5 minutes. Remove the cupcakes in their paper baking cups from the pan(s) to finish cooling on the rack.

Make the icing:

7. In a heavy large saucepan, combine the white chocolate, sugar, and cornstarch. Add the boiling water and stir until thickened over low heat. Cool to room temperature.

8. Using an electric mixer set at medium speed, cream the butter in a large bowl until light and fluffy. Gradually beat in the white chocolate mixture and continue beating until smooth. Using a metal spatula, spread some frosting on top of each cupcake. Refrigerate until the frosting sets and then loosely cover the cupcakes. Store in the refrigerator and bring to room temperature before serving.

Do ahead: The cupcakes can be made up to 1 day in advance or frozen up to 1 month.

MAKES 16 CUPCAKES.

Coconut Snowballs

These are great candies to present to white chocolate lovers during the holiday season.

Nougatine
⅔ cup sugar
½ teaspoon corn syrup
½ cup blanched sliced almonds

Snowballs
12 ounces finely chopped white
 chocolate, melted and tepid
2 cups sweetened shredded coconut

Dipping
1 pound finely chopped white
 chocolate

Make the nougatine:
 1. Line a baking sheet with parchment paper. In a heavy medium saucepan over high heat, melt the sugar and corn syrup, stirring constantly, until smooth. The sugar will caramelize and all lumps should be dissolved. (If sugar carmelizes too quickly and lumps remain, remove from heat and continue to stir until smooth.) Using a wooden spoon, stir in the almonds and coat them evenly with the mixture. Immediately pour the mixture onto the prepared baking sheet and cool completely. Break into 2-inch pieces.

Coarsely chop the nougatine in a food processor fitted with a metal blade, using on–off pulses.

Make the snowballs:

2.   In a large bowl, combine 1 cup of the nougatine with the melted white chocolate and the coconut. Set aside at room temperature until the mixture begins to harden, about 30 minutes. Roll into teaspoon-size balls.

3.   Line two baking sheets with parchment paper. In a double boiler over hot—not simmering—water, melt the white chocolate, stirring frequently. Let cool until tepid. Place the double boiler in front of you on the counter. Submerge one snowball in the melted white chocolate. Scoop out the snowball using a regular dinner fork and tap the snowball gently on the rim of the pan, allowing the excess white chocolate to drip back into the pan. Place the snowball on the prepared baking sheet. Repeat the process with the remaining snowballs. For a thicker coating, dip the snowballs again in the remaining melted white chocolate. Cool completely at room temperature until firm. Place each snowball in an appropriately sized paper or foil candy cup. Store in an airtight container at cool room temperature.

Do ahead: The snowballs can be made up to 2 weeks in advance.

MAKES 72 CANDIES.

White Chocolate–Coffee Truffles

White chocolate and coffee are a delightful flavor combination, as these beautiful truffles demonstrate. Note that the techniques used to dip the chocolate create a shiny finish without the extra work of tempering.

Truffles
2 tablespoons heavy (whipping)
  cream
1 tablespoon Kahlua or other coffee-
  flavored liqueur
1 tablespoon crème fraîche (see
  index)
6 ounces finely chopped white
  chocolate

2 teaspoons freshly ground coffee
  beans (fine grind)
Confectioners' sugar

Dipping
1 pound finely chopped white
  chocolate
Chocolate coffee bean candies

Make the truffles:

1.   In a heavy small saucepan over medium heat, bring the cream and Kahlua to a simmer, stirring frequently. Reduce the heat to low. Stir in the crème fraîche and mix until smooth; do not let the mixture boil. Add the white chocolate and ground coffee and whisk until smooth.

2.   Pour the mixture into a small bowl. Freeze until the mixture is firm enough to hold a shape, about 30 minutes.

3.   Line a baking sheet with waxed paper and dust generously with sugar. Spoon 10 mounds of the truffle mixture onto the prepared baking sheet, using about 2½ tablespoons of the truffle mixture for each. Freeze until the centers are almost firm, about 20 minutes.

4.   Roll each mound in sugar on the sheet, then roll between the palms of your hands into a smooth round. Set on another clean waxed paper-lined baking sheet and freeze at least 2 hours before dipping.

Dip the truffles:

5. In a double boiler over hot—not simmering—water, melt the white chocolate until a candy thermometer registers 115°F. As the chocolate melts and the water cools, replace the cool water with hot water, as needed.

6. Line a baking sheet with waxed paper. Place the double boiler on the counter in front of you. Submerge one truffle in the melted white chocolate (you may have to tilt the pan to completely submerge). Scoop out the truffle using a regular dinner fork, and tap the truffle gently on the rim of the pan, allowing the excess white chocolate to drip back into the pan. Gently drop the truffle onto the prepared baking sheet. Using your free hand, lightly press a coffee bean candy onto the center of the top of the truffle. Repeat the process with remaining truffles. (Note: Take the temperature of the white chocolate halfway through the dipping process to ensure that it is between 115°F and 120°F. If the temperature drops below 115°F, reheat chocolate by replacing water with hot water and stirring.) Refrigerate until the white chocolate is set, about 1 hour.

7. After the truffles are set, using rubber gloves or plastic wrap to prevent fingerprints, place in appropriately sized paper or foil candy cups. Arrange cups in an airtight container and refrigerate. Remove from the refrigerator about 30 minutes before serving.

Do ahead: The truffles can be made and refrigerated up to 1 week in advance, or frozen up to 2 months.

MAKES 10 TRUFFLES.

The creator: Sarah Tenaglia,
assistant editor for
Bon Appétit *magazine*

White Chocolate–Ginger Truffles

These truffles demonstrate how well the crisp, pungent flavor of ginger balances the sweetness of white chocolate. Note that there's no need to temper the dipping chocolate to achieve a professional finish.

Truffles
3 tablespoons plus 1 teaspoon heavy (whipping) cream
1 tablespoon crème fraîche (see index)
8 ounces finely chopped white chocolate

2 teaspoons minced crystallized (candied) ginger
Confectioners' sugar

Dipping
1 pound finely chopped white chocolate
Minced crystallized ginger (optional)

Make the truffles:

1.   In a heavy small saucepan over medium heat, bring the cream to a simmer, stirring frequently. Reduce the heat to low. Add the crème fraîche and stir until smooth; do not let boil. Stir in the white chocolate and the ginger until smooth.

2.   Pour the mixture into a small bowl. Freeze until the mixture is firm enough to hold a shape, about 20 minutes.

3.   Line a baking sheet with waxed paper and dust generously with sugar. Spoon 10 mounds onto the prepared baking sheet, using about 2½ tablespoons of the truffle mixture for each. Freeze until the centers are almost firm, about 30 minutes.

4.   Roll each mound in sugar on the sheet, then roll between the palms of your hands into a smooth round. Set on another clean waxed paper–lined baking sheet and freeze at least 2 hours before dipping.

Dip the truffles:

5.　In a double boiler over hot—not simmering—water, melt the white chocolate until it registers 115°F on a candy thermometer. As the chocolate melts and the water cools, replace the cool water with hot water, as needed.

6.　Line a baking sheet with waxed paper. Place the double boiler on the counter in front of you. Submerge one truffle in the melted white chocolate (you may have to tilt the pan to completely submerge). Scoop out the truffle using a regular dinner fork, and tap the truffle gently on the rim of the pan, allowing the excess white chocolate to drip back into the pan. Gently drop the truffle onto the prepared baking sheet. Using your free hand, lightly sprinkle the top with minced ginger, if desired. Repeat process with remaining truffles. (Note: Take the temperature of the white chocolate halfway through the dipping process to ensure that it is between 115°F and 120°F. If temperature drops below 115°F, reheat chocolate by replacing water with hot water and stirring.) Refrigerate until the white chocolate is set, about 1 hour.

8.　After the truffles are set, using rubber gloves or plastic wrap to prevent fingerprints, place the truffles in appropriately sized paper or foil candy cups. Arrange cups in an airtight container and refrigerate. Remove from refrigerator 30 minutes before serving.

Do ahead: The truffles can be made and refrigerated up to 1 week in advance, or frozen up to 2 months.

MAKES 10 TRUFFLES.

The creator: Sarah Tenaglia,
assistant editor for
Bon Appétit *magazine*

White Chocolate–Cointreau Truffles

Despite the smooth texture and delicate flavor, these truffles are simple to make and don't require tempering for a professional-appearing coating.

Truffles
*1 pound finely chopped white
    chocolate
1 cup heavy (whipping) cream
1 tablespoon Cointreau liqueur*

Dipping
*1 pound finely chopped white
    chocolate*

Make the truffles:

1.   Place the white chocolate in a heat-proof large bowl. In a heavy medium saucepan over medium-high heat, bring the cream to a full boil, stirring frequently. Pour the cream over the chocolate all at once and whisk until smooth. Whisk in the Cointreau. Let cool at room temperature for 30 minutes.

2.   Line baking sheets with waxed paper. Using 2 teaspoons or your palms (rinse and dry hands often), shape the white chocolate mixture into ¾-inch-diameter balls, using about 2 teaspoons of the mixture for each ball.

Place them about 1 inch apart on the prepared sheets. Refrigerate until chilled and firm, about 1 hour.

Dip the truffles:

3.   Line the baking sheets with clean waxed paper. In a double boiler over hot—not simmering—water, melt the remaining white chocolate, stirring frequently. Cool slightly. Submerge one truffle in the melted white chocolate. Scoop out the truffle using a regular dinner fork, and tap the truffle gently on the rim of the pan, allowing the excess white chocolate to drip back into the pan. Gently drop the truffle on the prepared sheet. Repeat the process with the remaining truffles. Let sit at room temperature until coating is firm, about 30 minutes. Cover and refrigerate at least 1 hour.

4.   After the truffles are set, place in appropriately sized paper or foil candy cups. Arrange the cups in an airtight container and refrigerate. Remove from the refrigerator about 30 minutes before serving.

Do ahead: The truffles can be made and refrigerated up to 1 week in advance, or frozen up to 2 months.

MAKES ABOUT 40 TRUFFLES.

*The creator: Jean Banchet,
chef/proprietor of Le Français
restaurant in Wheeling, Illinois*

White Chocolate Waffles with Brandied Cherries and Black Cherry Coulis

◁❧▷

These waffles can be served for brunch or dessert. They are crispy on the outside and soft and moist on the inside. Although their texture is homey, the flavor is pure sophistication. The batter must be made 1 day in advance, which makes it an ideal recipe for entertaining.

Waffles

4½ ounces white chocolate
1⅓ cups sifted flour
2 teaspoons baking powder
½ teaspoon cinnamon
⅛ teaspoon salt
6 tablespoons unsalted butter, at room temperature
½ cup sugar
2 large eggs, separated, at room temperature
½ cup milk

Coulis

1½ pounds black cherries
3 tablespoons sugar
3 tablespoons syrup from brandied Italian cherries in syrup*

Garnish

16 brandied Italian cherries in syrup*
8 ounces finely chopped white chocolate
1 cup heavy (whipping) cream, whipped and chilled

---

*Available at specialty food stores.

Make the waffles:

1.   Using a sharp knife, cut 2 ounces of the white chocolate into ½-inch squares. Set aside. Melt the remaining white chocolate, broken into squares, in a double boiler over hot—not simmering—water, stirring frequently. Keep lukewarm while preparing the batter.

2.   Sift the flour, baking powder, cinnamon, and salt together into a small bowl. Using an electric mixer set at medium-high speed, cream the butter and sugar together in a medium bowl until light and fluffy. Beat in the egg yolks, one at a time, beating well after each addition. Stir the melted white chocolate into the egg mixture. Heat milk to lukewarm and add in three parts, alternating with the sifted dry ingredients. Cover and refrigerate overnight.

Make the coulis:

3.   Stem and pit the black cherries and place in a blender or food processor fitted with a metal blade. Add the sugar and syrup from the brandied cherries. Puree and strain through a fine-mesh strainer into a bowl. Taste and add more sugar if needed.

Make the garnish:

4.   In a double boiler over hot—not simmering—water, melt the white chocolate, stirring frequently. Spread in a thin, even layer on a sheet of waxed paper. (It doesn't matter if edges are irregular.) Refrigerate the sheet of white chocolate until it hardens, about 1 hour.

Assemble:

5.   Bring the waffle batter to room temperature. Heat a waffle iron, preferably a round one. Drain the brandied cherries.

6.   Using an electric mixer set at low speed, beat the egg whites in a grease-free bowl until they start to foam. Gradually increase the speed to high. Continue beating until the egg whites form stiff, shiny peaks. Fold into the batter along with the reserved squares of white chocolate. Spoon into the preheated waffle iron. Cook the waffles until light golden brown, according to manufacturer's directions. (Waffles will still appear soft, but will become crisp after removal from the waffle iron. Do not overcook.)

7. If using a round waffle iron, arrange two quarters of waffle on each large dessert plate. (If using a square iron, cut waffles in half diagonally, and set two halves side by side, about an inch or two apart, on each large dessert plate.) Spoon some coulis between the waffles. Fill a pastry bag fitted with a star tip with the whipped cream. Pipe three rosettes on each plate: one on the pool of coulis and one on each waffle section. Place a brandied cherry on top of the rosettes on the waffles. Break the refrigerated white chocolate sheet into small, irregular pieces, and stick several into each rosette on the coulis in a free-form design. Serve immediately.

Do ahead: The batter can be refrigerated up to 2 days.

MAKES 6 TO 8 DESSERT SERVINGS.

The creator: Barbara Figueroa,
sous-chef of Chamelions restaurant
in Santa Monica, California,
contributing editor for Gastronome,
and editorial contributor to
The Wolfgang Puck Cookbook

9
Ice Cream, Frozen Desserts, and Beverages

White Chocolate Ice Cream

~~~
This is an exceptionally creamy ice cream and will not harden to the
degree of most homemade ones. It's the perfect choice for preparing white
chocolate milk shakes—although it's not too shabby when eaten straight
from the container, either.
~~~

¼ cup water
⅔ cup sugar
*12 ounces finely chopped white
    chocolate*
3 cups heavy (whipping) cream
*6 large egg yolks, at room
    temperature*

1. In a heavy medium saucepan over low heat, combine the water
and ⅓ cup of the sugar; stir constantly until the sugar dissolves. Increase
the heat to medium-high and bring the mixture to a boil, brushing down
the sugar crystals from the sides of the pan with water. Remove from heat
and whisk in the white chocolate, stirring until the mixture is smooth.

2. In a heavy medium saucepan over medium heat, bring the
cream to a boil. Remove from heat.

3. Using an electric mixer set at medium speed, beat the egg yolks
in a large bowl until light yellow. Gradually beat in the remaining sugar
and continue beating until mixture is thick and forms a ribbon when the
beaters are lifted. Beat in the white chocolate mixture, then the cream. Let
the mixture cool completely, stirring occasionally. Refrigerate until chilled,

about 30 minutes. Freeze the ice cream in an ice cream maker according to the manufacturer's instructions. Transfer the ice cream to a container, cover, and freeze.

Do ahead: The ice cream can be made up to 1 week in advance.

MAKES 1½ QUARTS.

White Chocolate–Ginger Ice Cream

Fresh ginger complements white chocolate like few other ingredients; its crisp, sharp flavor balances white chocolate's rich, sweet properties. This ice cream has an admirably smooth texture and delicate taste.

Ice cream
1 cup heavy (whipping) cream
1 cup milk
¼ cup sugar
¼ cup fresh grated, peeled ginger (about 2 ounces)
2 large egg yolks
5 ounces finely chopped white chocolate, melted and tepid

Garnish (optional)
Minced crystallized ginger
1 ounce white chocolate shavings (see index)

1.   In a heavy saucepan over low heat, slowly bring the cream, milk, sugar, and grated ginger to a boil, stirring occasionally. Immediately remove from heat. Let the ingredients steep together for 30 minutes.

2. In a small bowl, beat the egg yolks with the melted white chocolate. Whisk into the cream mixture. Strain the custard through a fine-mesh sieve or cheesecloth into a large bowl.

3. Pour the custard into an ice cream maker and freeze according to manufacturer's directions. Transfer the ice cream to a container, cover, and freeze.

4. Scoop ice cream into dessert bowls. Sprinkle with crystallized ginger and white chocolate shavings, if desired.

Do ahead: The ice cream can be made up to 3 days in advance.

MAKES 1 QUART.

*The creator: Daniel Thiebaut,
executive chef for The Mauna Kea
Beach Hotel in Kamuela, Hawaii*

Double White Chocolate Ice Cream

A celestial treat for white chocolate lovers: generous chunks of white chocolate are folded into freshly made white chocolate ice cream.

1 cup half-and-half
1 cup heavy (whipping) cream
10 ounces coarsely chopped white
   chocolate

2 large eggs, at room temperature
⅓ cup sugar

1. In a heavy medium saucepan over medium-high heat, bring the half-and-half and cream to a boil. Remove the pan from the heat. Add 6 ounces of the white chocolate and stir until melted and the mixture is smooth.

2. Using an electric mixer set at medium speed, beat the eggs in a double boiler over simmering water until pale yellow. Gradually add the sugar and beat until the mixture is thick and forms a ribbon when the beaters are lifted. Gradually stir in the white chocolate mixture and stir until the mixture coats the back of a spoon and leaves a clear path when a finger is run across it. Remove from the heat and cool to room temperature, stirring occasionally.

3. Refrigerate until well chilled, about 2 hours. Freeze the ice cream in an ice cream maker according to manufacturer's instructions. Transfer the ice cream to a container and fold in the remaining white chocolate chunks. Cover and freeze.

Do ahead: The ice cream can be made up to 1 week in advance.

MAKES 1½ PINTS.

White Chocolate Sherbet

This simple-to-make sherbet possesses a distinct white chocolate flavor. It's a most refreshing summer treat, as it's not as rich as ice cream.

2 cups sugar
1½ cups water

8 ounces finely chopped white
    chocolate
Fresh raspberries, for garnish

1. In a heavy medium saucepan over low heat, combine the sugar and water; stir until the sugar dissolves. Increase the heat to medium-high and boil the syrup, brushing down the sugar crystals from the sides of the pan with water, until the mixture registers 238°F on a candy thermometer.

2. Meanwhile, in a double boiler over hot—not simmering—water, melt the white chocolate, stirring frequently. Stir into the sugar syrup until smooth. Refrigerate, stirring occasionally, until chilled, about 2 hours. Freeze the sherbet in an ice cream maker according to manufacturer's instructions. Transfer the sherbet to a container, cover, and freeze. Serve in tulip glasses with raspberries, if desired.

Do ahead: The sherbet can be made up to 2 days in advance.

MAKES 1 QUART.

*The creator: Alain Roby, former
pastry chef for Vista International
Hotel in New York, New York*

Winter White Pie

Thanks to white chocolate, this dessert tastes as rich and creamy as ice cream. Actually, it may remind you of a DoveBar—presented in a pie shell. Use your imagination when decorating the pie with the semisweet chocolate; you can create quite a dramatic effect if you let the pieces jut flamboyantly out of the top.

4 ounces finely chopped semisweet chocolate, melted
¼ cup water
6 ounces finely chopped white chocolate
2 large eggs, separated, at room temperature
1 cup heavy (whipping) cream, chilled
½ cup sugar
1 baked 9-inch deep pie crust (see index)

1. Line two baking sheets with waxed paper. Draw one 7-inch and one 8-inch diameter circle on one baking sheet. Brush a ⅛-inch-thick layer of the melted semisweet chocolate over each circle. Spread the remaining chocolate in a thin layer over the other prepared baking sheet in no particular shape. Refrigerate the chocolate on the waxed paper until it is firm, about 20 minutes. Break the last, unshaped layer of dark chocolate into 2- to 3-inch pieces.

2. In a saucepan over high heat, bring the water to a boil. Remove from heat and add the white chocolate, stirring constantly until melted. Let the mixture cool for 30 minutes. Whisk in the egg yolks.

3. Using an electric mixer set at low speed, beat the egg whites in a grease-free small bowl until they start to foam. Gradually increase the speed to high and continue beating until the egg whites start to form soft peaks. Gradually beat in ¼ cup of the sugar and continue beating the egg whites until they form stiff, shiny peaks.

4. Using an electric mixer set at medium speed, whip the cream in a large bowl until slightly thickened. Gradually beat in the remaining sugar and continue beating until the cream is nearly stiff. Fold one-fourth of the egg whites into the cool white chocolate mixture to lighten it; fold in the remaining egg whites. Fold one-fourth of the whipped cream into the white chocolate mixture; fold in the remaining whipped cream.

5. Spoon a little less than one-third of the mousse in the cool, baked pie shell. Smooth the top with a spatula. Top with the 7-inch dark chocolate disk. Spread with half of the remaining mousse, and top with the 8-inch semisweet chocolate disk. Top with the remaining mousse, smoothing the top with a spatula. Freeze for 1 hour. Arrange the broken pieces of semisweet chocolate to jut out of the top of the pie. Freeze, covered, at least 6 hours. Slice while frozen, and serve immediately.

Do ahead: The pie can be made up to 2 days in advance.

MAKES 8 SERVINGS.

The creator: KT Burdon, an East Hampton, New York, caterer

White Chocolate Chip–Mint Glacé

This dessert is denser than ice cream. I love the crunch of the white chocolate chips—it's the perfect foil to the smooth glacé. The fresh mint flavor is subtle yet refreshing.

2 cups sugar
2 cups water
6 tablespoons chopped fresh mint
6 large egg yolks, at room
   temperature
2 cups chilled heavy (whipping)
   cream, whipped
½ cup plus 2 tablespoons white
   chocolate chips
Fresh mint leaves, for garnish
   (optional)

1.   Line a 9″ × 5″ loaf pan with enough plastic wrap to overhang the edges and enclose the filling completely. In a heavy large saucepan over high heat, combine the sugar, water, and mint; stir until the sugar dissolves. Increase heat to medium-high and boil the syrup, brushing down sugar crystals from side of pan with water until mixture registers 238°F on a candy thermometer.

2.   Meanwhile, using a heavy-duty mixer set at medium speed, beat the egg yolks until they become pale yellow and form a thick ribbon when

the beaters are lifted. Strain the syrup into a small bowl. Slowly beat the hot syrup into the yolks and continue beating until the mixture is cool. Fold the whipped cream into the egg yolk mixture. Fold in the white chocolate chips.

    3.   Gently spoon into the prepared pan. Fold plastic over the filling and freeze for at least 8 hours. Uncover and invert the pan onto a serving platter and peel off the plastic wrap. Cut the glacé into slices. Garnish with fresh mint leaves, if desired.

Do ahead: The glacé can be made up to 2 days in advance.

MAKES 10 SERVINGS.

The creator: Greg Waldron,
former executive chef for the
Hotel Hana-Maui in Hana, Hawaii

White Chocolate Frozen Soufflé

The texture of this dessert is flawless; it's exceptionally smooth and creamy.

5 large egg yolks, at room temperature
½ cup plus 2 tablespoons sugar
2 tablespoons water
1 teaspoon corn syrup
3 ounces finely chopped white chocolate, melted and tepid
¼ cup kirsch
2 cups heavy (whipping) cream, whipped
Semisweet or bittersweet chocolate shavings or curls (see index)

1. Using a heavy-duty mixer set at medium speed, beat the egg yolks and 2 tablespoons of sugar in a large bowl until the mixture becomes pale yellow and forms a thick ribbon when the beaters are lifted.

2. In a heavy small saucepan over medium heat, combine the remaining sugar, water, and corn syrup; stir until the sugar dissolves. Increase the heat to medium-high and boil the syrup, brushing down sugar crystals from the sides of the pan with water, until it registers 238°F on a candy thermometer. Using a heavy-duty mixer set at medium-high speed,

slowly pour the syrup in a steady stream into the egg yolk mixture, beating constantly.

3.   Cool the egg yolk mixture to lukewarm and add it to the melted white chocolate in three parts.

4.   When the mixture is cool, fold in the kirsch and whipped cream. Carefully spoon into eight 1-cup custard cups, cover with plastic wrap, and freeze overnight or for at least several hours.

5.   Transfer to the refrigerator 30 minutes before serving. Garnish each cup with chocolate shavings or a chocolate curl.

Do ahead: The frozen soufflé can be made up to three days ahead.

MAKES 8 SERVINGS.

*The creator: Piet Wigmans,
executive chef for the Mauna Lani
Bay Hotel in Hawaii*

White Chocolate–Chestnut Parfait with Cranberry-Champagne Coulis

This parfait is filled with fall flavors, making it ideal to serve throughout the holiday season. The flavor is well balanced; the sweetness of the white chocolate is tempered by the unsweetened chestnut puree, and the fruitiness of the cranberries in the coulis is enhanced by that of the champagne.

Terrine
3 large egg yolks, at room temperature
½ cup sugar
2 tablespoons water
8 ounces finely chopped white chocolate, melted and tepid
4 large egg whites, at room temperature
2 cups heavy (whipping) cream, chilled

Filling
4 ounces semisweet chocolate, melted
½ cup unsweetened chestnut puree
4 large egg yolks
2 cups heavy (whipping) cream, chilled

Coulis
1½ cups sugar
1½ cups water
1½ cups cranberries
1½ cups extra-dry or brut champagne

Make the parfait:

1.   In a double boiler over simmering water, combine the egg yolks, 4 tablespoons of the sugar, and water, and whisk until the mixture doubles in volume. Fold the melted white chocolate into the egg yolk mixture and

194

remove from heat. Transfer the mixture into a large bowl. Let stand for 1 hour.

2.   Using an electric mixer set at low speed, beat the egg whites in a grease-free medium bowl until they start to foam. Gradually increase the speed to high and continue beating the egg whites until they form soft peaks. Gradually beat in the remaining sugar and continue beating the egg whites until they form stiff peaks. Fold the egg whites into the white chocolate mixture; fold in the whipped cream.

Make the filling:

3.   In a large bowl, mix the semisweet chocolate with the chestnut puree and egg yolks. Using an electric mixer set at medium speed, whip the cream in a large chilled bowl until nearly stiff. Fold into the chestnut mixture. Cover and refrigerate for 1 hour.

Assemble the parfait:

4.   Line a 12″ × 3″ × 3″ pan with enough plastic wrap to overhang edges and enclose the filling completely. Spoon half of the white chocolate mixture evenly into the prepared pan. Freeze for 30 minutes. Top with the chestnut filling and cover with the remaining white chocolate mixture. Fold plastic over to cover parfait and freeze at least 8 hours or overnight.

Make the coulis:

5.   In a medium saucepan over medium-high heat, combine the sugar and water. When it begins to simmer, add the cranberries and cook until soft, stirring frequently, about 5 to 10 minutes. Puree mixture in a blender or food processor fitted with a metal blade. Strain through a fine-mesh sieve into a large saucepan. Place over high heat, add champagne, and boil until thickened to sauce consistency, stirring frequently, about 5 to 10 minutes. Cool to room temperature.

Assemble:

6.   Uncover and invert the pan onto a serving plate and carefully peel off the plastic wrap. Slightly soften in the refrigerator, about 2 hours. Cut the parfait into 1-inch slices. Spoon some of the coulis onto each dessert plate and top with a slice of parfait.

Do ahead: The parfait and the sauce can be made up to 2 days ahead. Bring the sauce to room temperature before serving.

MAKES 12 SERVINGS.

The creators: John Makin, executive chef, and Mario G. Lara, assistant pastry chef, for The Remington in Houston, Texas

Frozen Almond Cream

This easy-to-make frozen dessert combines creamy and crunchy attributes for a true textural treat.

1 cup heavy (whipping cream)
1 5-ounce bar Nestlé® Alpine White™ with Almonds, finely chopped and divided
2 teaspoons amaretto
2 large egg whites
2 tablespoons sugar

1. Line 12 muffin cups with foil baking cups. In a heavy small saucepan over medium heat, scald ¼ cup of the cream; remove from heat. Add ½ cup finely chopped white chocolate and the amaretto; stir until melted.

2. Transfer to a large bowl; cool until tepid. Using an electric mixer set at low speed, beat the egg whites in a grease-free small bowl until they start to foam. Gradually increase the speed to high and continue beating the egg whites until they form soft peaks. Gradually beat in the sugar and continue beating the egg whites until they form stiff peaks. Fold one-fourth of the beaten egg whites into the white chocolate mixture to lighten it; fold in the remaining egg whites.

3. Using an electric mixer set at medium-high speed, beat the remaining ¾ cup cream in a small bowl until stiff. Fold the cream into the white chocolate mixture. Fold in ¼ cup of the chopped white chocolate. Spoon an equal amount into each of the prepared muffin cups. Sprinkle an equal amount of the remaining chopped white chocolate over each cup. Cover and freeze until firm, at least 8 hours or overnight.

Do ahead: The almond creams can be made up to 3 days in advance.

MAKES 12 SERVINGS.

Hot White Chocolate

A cup of haute, hot white chocolate will soothe any soul on a rainy day.

Hot Chocolate
2 cups milk
*2 ounces finely chopped white
    chocolate*
1 large egg white

Garnish
Whipped cream
White chocolate shavings (see index)

1.   In a heavy medium saucepan over medium heat, combine the milk and white chocolate, stirring frequently, until smooth.

2.   Increase the heat to high and bring the mixture to a gentle boil. Remove the pan from heat.

3.   In a small bowl, beat the egg white until frothy. Using an electric mixer, gradually beat it into the white chocolate mixture. Return the mixture to the saucepan over low heat and stir for 1 minute. Pour an equal amount of the mixture into two mugs and top each serving with a dollop of whipped cream and a sprinkle of white chocolate shavings. Serve immediately.

MAKES 2 SERVINGS.

White Chocolate Cappuccino

This recipe is a variation of a creamy, rich cappuccino served at L'Ermitage Hotel in Beverly Hills. Their secret ingredient is ice cream; mine is making it with white chocolate ice cream. Increase the ingredients proportionally for more servings.

1 scoop (⅓ cup) white chocolate ice
   cream (see index)
¾ cup freshly brewed espresso (may
   use decaffeinated)
¼ cup milk
White chocolate shavings (see index)

1. In a heavy small saucepan over medium heat, combine the ice cream and espresso, stirring occasionally, until the ice cream melts.
2. In an espresso/cappuccino machine, steam the milk. (Or, bring the milk to a boil in a heavy small saucepan.) Pour the ice cream mixture into a blender and mix until frothy.
3. Pour the ice cream mixture into a large cup or mug. Mix in the steamed milk, including any froth. Top with white chocolate shavings. Serve immediately.

MAKES 1 SERVING.

White Chocolate Milkshake

Add 2 teaspoons of malted milk powder for a sensational malt. Or, make a raspberry–white chocolate milkshake: puree and strain ½ pint of fresh raspberries, and add them to the shake with sugar and raspberry liqueur to taste.

6 tablespoons milk
2 tablespoons half-and-half
1 pint white chocolate ice cream (see
   index)

In a blender or a food processor fitted with a metal blade, process the milk, half-and-half, and ice cream until smooth, about 1 minute. Pour into a tall glass and serve immediately.

MAKES 1 16-OUNCE SERVING.

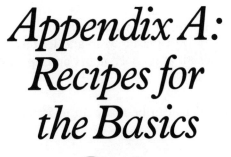

Appendix A: Recipes for the Basics

Crème Fraîche

1 cup heavy (whipping) cream
2 tablespoons buttermilk

In a glass jar, measuring cup, or bowl, combine the cream and the buttermilk. Cover loosely with plastic wrap and let rest at room temperature until thickened, at least 12 hours and up to 24. Cover tightly and refrigerate.

Do ahead: The crème fraîche can be made up to 1 week in advance.

Genoise

This is, quite simply, one of the finest genoise recipes I've encountered.

4 large eggs, at room temperature
⅔ cup sugar
½ teaspoon vanilla extract
1¼ cups sifted cake flour
4 tablespoons unsalted butter, melted
  and tepid

1.   Position a rack in the center and preheat oven to 350°F. Lightly butter an 8-inch round cake pan and line the bottom with parchment paper. Lightly butter the parchment. Dust the bottom and sides of the pan with flour; tap out the excess. In a medium saucepan over low heat, whisk the eggs and sugar together until lukewarm. Transfer the egg mixture to a large bowl. Using an electric mixer set at high speed, beat the egg mixture until it cools and becomes very thick, about 5 minutes. Stir in the vanilla.

2.   Fold in the flour and the butter. Spread the batter evenly into the prepared cake pan and bake until a tester inserted in the center of the cake comes out clean and the cake shrinks slightly from the sides of the pan, about 35 minutes. Transfer the cake in the pan to a wire rack to cool completely. Invert the cake onto the rack. (Note: If the cake doesn't come out of the pan easily, place the bottom of the cake pan over low heat on the stove for about 30 seconds, and then invert.)

Do ahead: The genoise can be made and refrigerated up to 2 days in advance, or frozen up to 1 month.

MAKES ONE 8-INCH GENOISE.

The creator: Roy Yamaguchi,
chef/proprietor of Roy's restaurant
in Honolulu, Hawaii

Pie Crust

2 cups flour
½ teaspoon salt
¼ pound unsalted butter, cut into 8
pieces, chilled

3 tablespoons vegetable shortening
5 to 6 tablespoons ice-cold water

1. In a food processor fitted with a metal blade, combine the flour and salt. Add the butter and shortening, and process, using on–off pulses, until the mixture resembles coarse meal.

2. With the machine running, add enough water through the feed tube, 1 tablespoon at a time, just until the mixture begins to form a dough. Do not overprocess.

3. Using a rubber spatula, transfer the dough to a sheet of plastic wrap. Wrap the dough and shape into a ball, then a flat disc. Refrigerate at least 1 hour or up to 2 days.

To blind bake (precook the pie crust):

1. Let the dough soften for a couple of minutes on a floured surface. Roll out the dough to ⅛-inch thickness and about 11 or 12 inches in diameter.

2. Roll the dough loosely around a rolling pin and unroll into a 9- or 10-inch pie pan. Gently pat into the pan, allowing the excess dough to hang over the edges. Trim the dough so that it overhangs 1 inch from the pan edge. Fold the dough edges under and crimp to form a high border. Prick the bottom of the dough with a fork. Cover with plastic wrap and refrigerate for at least 30 minutes or overnight.

3. Position a rack in the center and preheat oven to 375°F. Line the pie crust with aluminum foil and fill to the top of the crust with pie weights or dried beans. Bake until the sides of the pie crust are firm, about 15 minutes. Remove the foil and weights and continue baking until the

crust is firm and brown, about 15 minutes. Transfer in the pan to a wire rack to cool.

MAKES ONE 9- OR 10-INCH PIE CRUST.

Easy White Chocolate Decorations

Quick White Chocolate Curls

Use at least a large bar of white chocolate, although a larger block of white chocolate is preferable. Be sure it is at room temperature. Place a sheet of waxed paper on the work surface. Using a swivel-blade vegetable peeler, make the curls by pressing firmly down the smooth side of the white chocolate. The firmer the pressure, the thicker the curl. Allow curls to fall onto the waxed paper. Refrigerate in an airtight container until needed. (Use a fork or other utensil to transfer curls to the dessert, or they might melt from the temperature of your hands.) Another option is to simply let the curls drop directly from the bar onto the dessert.

White Chocolate Shavings

Use at least a large bar of white chocolate, although a larger block of white chocolate is preferable. Be sure it is at room temperature. Place a sheet of waxed paper on the work surface. Draw a knife at an angle along the smooth side of the white chocolate, allowing the shavings to fall onto the waxed paper. Or, use a swivel-blade vegetable peeler and make quick, short strokes, allowing the shavings to fall onto the waxed paper.

White Chocolate Leaves

Use firm, clean, nonpoisonous leaves such as citrus, camelia, or gardenia. Melt a small amount (2 to 4 ounces) of white chocolate and cool to tepid. Line a baking sheet with waxed paper. Using a metal spatula or the back of a spoon, spread the white chocolate thinly and evenly over the underside of a leaf. Remove excess white chocolate from the edges of the leaf. Repeat the process with the remaining leaves. Place leaves, white chocolate side up, on the prepared baking sheet and refrigerate until firm. Gently peel away the leaf from the white chocolate. Use immediately, or transfer the white chocolate leaves to an airtight container and refrigerate until ready to use.

Bonaparte Pastry Baskets

These crisp, delicate baskets provide an elegant way to present your favorite white chocolate mousse. You'll need 2 cups of mousse to fill 8 baskets.

6 sheets of filo dough
8 tablespoons unsalted butter, melted
2 tablespoons confectioners' sugar

1. Position a rack in the center and preheat oven to 400°F.
2. Lay 1 sheet of filo dough on a dry, flat surface. Lightly brush the filo with some of the melted butter, and sprinkle with 1 teaspoon of the

confectioners' sugar. Top with a second sheet of filo, lightly brush with some of the butter, and sprinkle with 1 teaspoon of the confectioners' sugar. Repeat with a third sheet of filo.

3.   Using a sharp knife, cut the stacked filo dough into four 6-inch squares. Place one square into each of four 6-ounce unbuttered custard cups. Gently press the center of the squares into the cups to shape a free-form basket. Repeat the process with the remaining filo dough, butter, and sugar, and four more custard cups. Place the cups into a shallow baking pan.

4.   Bake until golden brown, about 8 to 10 minutes. Transfer the cups in the pan to a wire rack to cool completely. Gently remove the filo from the cups. Store in an airtight container at room temperature.

Do ahead: The baskets can be made up to 1 day in advance.

MAKES 8 BASKETS.

The creator: Raymond Haldeman,
president of Raymond Haldeman
Restaurant/Catering in
Philadelphia, Pennsylvania

Toasted Nuts

Place the nuts in a single layer on a baking sheet and bake in an oven set at 350°F until golden brown in color, about 5 to 10 minutes.

To skin and toast hazelnuts: Place the nuts in a single layer on a baking sheet and bake in an oven set at 350°F until the skins begin to split and the nuts turn golden under the skins, about 8 to 12 minutes. Transfer the nuts to a clean dish towel, wrap, and let cool for 20 minutes. Use the towel to rub off the skins.

Appendix B:
Cooking Schools
and
White Chocolate
Sources

Cooking Schools

In order to further explore the subject of white chocolate, it's helpful to study the subject with culinary experts. Unfortunately, I have not been able to discover any classes which focus solely on white chocolate. However, the following schools offer comprehensive, intensive chocolate courses and promise to devote some of their curriculum to white chocolate. They also indicate that with enough demand, they may custom-tailor courses to suit white chocolate devotees.

International Pastry Arts Center
357 Adams Street
Bedford Hills, NY 10507
(914) 666-2325

Peter Kump's New York Cooking School
307 E. 92nd Street
New York, NY 10128
(212) 410-4601

St. Moritz Swiss Confectionery School
350 N. Canon Drive
Beverly Hills, CA 90210
(213) 859-7672

Cacao Barry Training Center
1500 Suckle Highway
Pennsauken, NJ 08110
(609) 488-2255

For Further Study

Richardson Researches, Inc.
23449 Foley Street
Hayward, CA 94545
(415) 785-1350
Classes offered stress confectionary technology and are geared for those who seek a professional career in chocolate manufacturing.

Palatex Inc.
311 E. 46th Street, 5th Floor
New York, NY 10017
(212) 319-6868
This food and beverage testing and research firm offers classes on the evaluation of chocolate and the development of tasting skills.

Sources

In case you have difficulty locating a particular brand of white chocolate, the following are some of the companies offering mail-order sources:

Valrhona Ivoire:
Marcel Akselrod Company
530 W. 25th Street
New York, NY 10001
(212) 675-7777

Callebaut White Couverture:
S. E. Rykoff & Company
P.O. Box 21467
Los Angeles, CA 90021
(213) 624-6094 *or* (800) 421-9873

Callebaut White Couverture, Lindt Blancor,
Williams-Sonoma White Baking Chips (made by Valrhona):
Williams-Sonoma
Mail Order Department
P.O. Box 3792
San Francisco, CA 94120-7456
(415) 652-9007

Carma Ivory:
Albert Uster Imports Inc.
P.O. Box 770
Gaithersburg, MD 20877
(800) 231-8154

Fred's White Chips:
Leppla Enterprises Inc.
P.O. Box 20307
Oakland, CA 94620
(415) 655-2196

Nestlé Snowcap® Coating:
Maid of Scandinavia
3244 Raleigh Avenue
Minneapolis, MN 55416
(800) 328-6722 *or* (612) 927-7996

Cacao Barry Chocolat Blanc:
Assouline & Ting, Inc.
926 W. Allegheny Avenue
Philadelphia, PA 19133
(800) 521-4491; (212) 496-0577;
(215) 225-8600 (west of Mississippi)

Index